For

Mum and Dad who together showed me
what is important in life.

Megan Oakley Howell
my best friend and wife.

My beautiful daughter Amelie.

Root

Rob
Howell

photography
by Alexander J. Collins

BLOOMSBURY ABSOLUTE

LONDON · OXFORD · NEW YORK · NEW DELHI · SYDNEY

contents

Foreword by
Josh Eggleton

A foreword of sorts, a small story and a love letter...

Before we start the story, I first want to say that Root the restaurant belongs to Rob and Meg and would not exist, or be what it is, without them. They are its soul and beating heart and it gives me great pleasure to be asked to write this foreword.

Can I call them my protégés? It feels weird to me, but I guess they are. They are one of the most important parts of our restaurant and hospitality family. We have been working together for ten years. They both started at the Pony & Trap and showed great promise from day dot. We slogged it out there together for years and also went on to cook as guests in restaurants all over the UK and further afield. We found ourselves in huge pop up restaurants and food festivals. Most importantly we ate and drank together in pursuit of the perfect meal.

The eventual culmination of all of these food experiences was Root the restaurant – a simple concept, an idea I dreamt up driving to work one day. But more on that later.

Life in this restaurant is created from Rob and Meg's experiences. They have the given knack to create perfect hospitality from within our quirky little sea container restaurant on the Bristol dockside. And all of us have learnt a great deal from their example. It is a great feeling to know that we are learning together and from each other in our kitchen classroom.

I guess in reality Root was borne out of a failure on my part. We had opened Chicken Shed – with everything we do we try to project a subtle message! The thinking behind Chicken Shed was cooking sustainable organic, high welfare chicken, using the whole bird with no waste. I love fried chicken but wanted to do it properly. It turned out that our supply of good fried chicken generally did not come from a high welfare bird – the legs had done far too much work. So, being unable to maintain a constant supply of the right standard of chicken combined with a struggle to maintain enthusiasm amongst the staff, maintaining customer interest and controlling the quality of the food led to something having to change. And having to change fast!

One day it hit me. All this chicken was crazy, maybe we all eat too much meat. I hardly eat meat at home so what were we doing in this business? So, we decided to open a restaurant with vegetables as the star of the show, with a small amount of protein on the side as an option. I wrote one menu and showed it to Rob. First thing he said was, can I change this? Of course, you can! Was it my opening menu? Was it hell? It was it littered with our DNA? Yes, of course, but now it had its own.

We told no one we were going to change from Chicken Shed to Root. We finished one Saturday evening and spent two and half days decorating and changing the logos and opened the following Tuesday evening. Everyone showed up for chicken, but we only had vegetables.

It's fair to say the business exploded. I've cooked in Bristol for 20 years and have never seen that happen – and the amazing standards only ever get better.

The recipes in this book are a reflection of Rob's life work and I'm so proud to have been a part of it. This will be a book for life and will cement itself into one of the classics. You will be able to use the recipes over and over or just simply learn some of the simple preparations that bring the dishes together. It is a great education in how to get maximum flavour out of vegetables. In my opinion vegetables taste better than anything else – you just need to know how to cook them. Root will show you how.

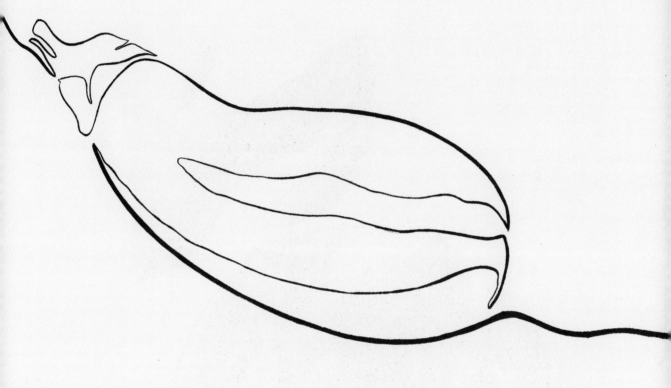

introduction

I have been lucky enough to have had people around me throughout my life who have made food a joy.

Growing up, my sister, brother and I enjoyed delicious home-cooked meals which were eaten as a family around the kitchen table every night. At weekends, wonderful roast dinners were placed before us to enjoy and relish. Looking back, I really don't know how mum did it!

Our annual summer holidays were spent in the north of France. Though very young, perhaps five or six, I can clearly remember the wonderful time spent visiting the local shops for special treats and shopping at the *supermarché* gathering provisions for the days ahead. I was fast becoming fascinated by the many exotic local delicacies of Normandy and Brittany; the amazing cuts of meat in the butcher, the glistening shellfish at the dockside, the snapping of the crabs and lobsters in the fishmonger and the preparation of the freshly caught wriggling eels. Waiting for July to come around, to get back on that ferry across the channel, each year more special than the last with another regional delicacy on our minds. But my culinary fascinations had their limits at that age and so I tended to play it safe with an endless supply of filled baguettes!

At the age of 14 I started working in a local restaurant on Friday and Saturday evenings and for Sunday lunch, plating starters and desserts. After leaving school I went to catering collage for a year and then secured a full time job under chef Adam Fellows at Goodfellows. My first year was spent helping in the patisserie section alongside the talented Gunther Repper. I started my working day at 5am and finished in the afternoon, making everything from pastries to bread, operas to lemon tarts – and I loved it. I then moved over to the fish section in the small open kitchen, working alongside Adam Fellows and Adam Dwyer. To this day I still have the little the notebook in which I would write up the recipes and plan our menus.

After two years at Goodfellows I took myself off to London to work under French chef Pascal Proyart. My six-month spell under Proyart taught me not only about life in a full-on professional kitchen but also about full-on life! Working in a brigade of 12 chefs, most of whom were at least ten years older than me, was tough and challenging but ultimately rewarding. The passion the guys showed and the sheer hard work they put in was inspiring. I once watched three of the Italian chefs cooking a staff dinner with just a few fish scraps – they made a wonderful fresh pasta with a sauce of olive oil, chilli, garlic and red mullet off cuts. Watching them make the pasta and then using the pasta water to make an emulsion was a revelation. It was one of the best dishes I had ever tasted, and I remember thinking that this was proper cooking and that I really needed to learn how to become a proper cook. And so I went to France to work in a hotel kitchen in the French Alps for a season.

With my six-month stage in France over, I headed back to the UK and got myself a job in Edinburgh to work for another legendary chef, Roy Brett at Ondine. In Roy's kitchen I became a real chef, confident and creative. I learned the importance of using the freshest of ingredients and how simplicity is the best friend to flavour. The passion and dedication of everyone in the restaurant was inspiring. The ability and the luxury to use the very best Scottish produce was a thrill. As young chefs we would spend all of our time cooking at work together and then cooking and eating at home together. I made friends at Ondine to last a lifetime.

I loved Edinburgh, Ondine, my friends and my social life, but I missed home and my family. Though growing up not far from Bristol, I was relatively unfamiliar with the city. I had heard of a pub just outside Bristol winning a Michelin star so I made contact asking if there might be a job going. They said there was and so two weeks later I was back living with my parents and working at the legendary Pony & Trap as a junior sous chef.

Working at the Pony & Trap for six years alongside owner and chef Josh Eggleton made me the chef I am today. At the age of 21, I became Head Chef, retaining the Michelin star which is held to this day. I made many friends there and learned cooking skills that would last a lifetime. It was also where I met my beautiful wife Megan.

While in Bristol I also got the chance to work at the outstanding Ethicurean. The Ethicurean Restaurant is tucked away in a Victorian walled garden with the most amazing views of the Mendip Hills. The Pennington brothers are serving modern British food in a beautiful location with a forward-thinking ethical approach. Watching the seasons come and go right in front of your eyes, and seeing the amount of work and care Mark the gardener put into growing produce, gave me a new-found respect for growers, producers and the vegetables themselves. Working alongside Matthew, Iain, Rich and Billy I was taught a whole new approach to cooking and preserving, and what a game changer it was.

This is the culinary journey which took me from family meals around our kitchen table to Head Chef at Root in Bristol, working hand in hand with Megan.

The idea that one day I would write a cookbook and that it would be published was nothing more than a distant dream. The dream is now a reality and if my book can get others to cook alongside friends and loved ones as I used to with my mum, and if new food horizons are discovered then I will feel that a job has been well done.

Happy cooking!

Root & the
Root cookbook

As I write this in the summer of 2020, Root has been open for a little over three years. We opened with the mission of creating a vegetable-led restaurant, neither vegan nor vegetarian, that would include on the menu a little fish, game and meat but with the explicit and stated aim of cooking vegetables brilliantly and making them the star of our new culinary show. This is the book of our show and it is a record of our recipes. Many of the dishes happen to be vegan or can be made vegan with simple adjustments. There is some meat and fish in here and, of course, desserts, but mostly vegetables.

The cooking at Root has become more pared down over the years. Perhaps not surprising given that Root is a restaurant based in a shipping container! We have two induction hobs, a fryer, a chargrill and an old oven. It is in essence a domestic kitchen. We usually only have two or three elements on the plate – the direct result of using just a few excellent ingredients and cooking them with minimal equipment in our minimalist kitchen in order to create something completely delicious. And so it is that the recipes in this book require no fancy kitchen gadgets or 'chef's toys'; they are simple to make, easy to assemble and wonderful to eat. These are the dishes that have been on our menu since opening and which have become firm favourites with our customers.

Food brings people together and is a constant joy. The recipes in this book will, I hope, open minds to the wonders of a vegetable-led diet, packed with wonderful flavours, and also help change people's thinking about how best to eat our way through life. Indeed, there are few things you really need for a life well lived but good food is definitely one of them.

Seasonality

In this day and age, it is so easy to talk about seasonality and sustainability but less easy to practise it, especially when confronted by the shelves in your local supermarket where everything is available all the year round, shiny, pristine and perfect. Why would you not eat asparagus from January through to December? Yet once you start eating with the focus on supporting local producers, farmers, markets and grocers, you will soon discover the deep benefits of adhering to the seasons. Put simply, everything tastes better when in season. And yes, you will discover that there is nothing better than the first asparagus of the year, the early British tomatoes and the broad beans of high summer.

Cooking with the seasons allows vegetables to be showcased at their best. Winter calls for heavier heartier meals built around root vegetables perhaps. Spring brings fresh green vegetables to the table while summer displays all the colours in the rainbow and more. Autumn heralds mushrooms, berries and fruits, and then the year starts again and with it the glories of another round of wonderful seasonal produce to enjoy.

Seasonal favourites to look out for

All year round	Winter	Spring	Summer	Autumn
Beetroot	Apples and pears	Asparagus	Aubergines	Blackberries/
Cabbages	Sprouts	Broccoli	Summer berries	brambles
Carrots	Chestnuts	Elderflower	Brand beans	Plums
Cauliflower	Jerusalem	Kohl rabi	Courgettes	Quince
Celeriac	artichokes	New potatoes	Cucumber	Squashes and
Garlic	Kale	Spring onions	Peas	pumpkins
Leeks	Parsnips	Watercress	Salad leaves	Leeks
Mushrooms (either	Forced rhubarb	Wild garlic	Sweetcorn	
wild or cultivated)	Salsify		Tomatoes	
Radishes	Swede			
	Turnips			

Produce

Produce is all about quality, quality, quality. Fruit, vegetables, meat, fish, game, dairy, spices, vinegars, oils. Though you will spend a little more in your search for excellence, the extra expense will prove well worth it. Down in the West Country we are blessed with being surrounded by so many amazingly passionate growers and producers. My mantra is a simple one – buy little and buy often and get to know your producers so that you can discover that extraordinary something that makes their produce so special. Follow this simple rule and you will make food friends for life!

Seasoning

Season, season and then check the seasoning again. You can follow a recipe to the last letter but without due care and attention to seasoning your dish will always fall short. I remember when, as a young chef in the kitchen on a busy Saturday night, the Head Chef came over and asked me, 'Is it seasoned?' 'Well, I put a pinch of salt and pepper in it so yes chef.' He tasted it and shouted at me 'No it's not!' The lesson learned was a simple one – the more often you taste your food when cooking, the more quickly you will learn about how to season and how to bring out all the wonderful flavours in the dish.

It took me a while into my professional career before I fully understood that seasoning didn't just mean salt and pepper, but also fat, acid and heat. Balancing the seasoning of a dish – sweet, spicy, sour, creamy, salty is crucial to the overall success of a dish. Learn to season and you will have learned how to cook!

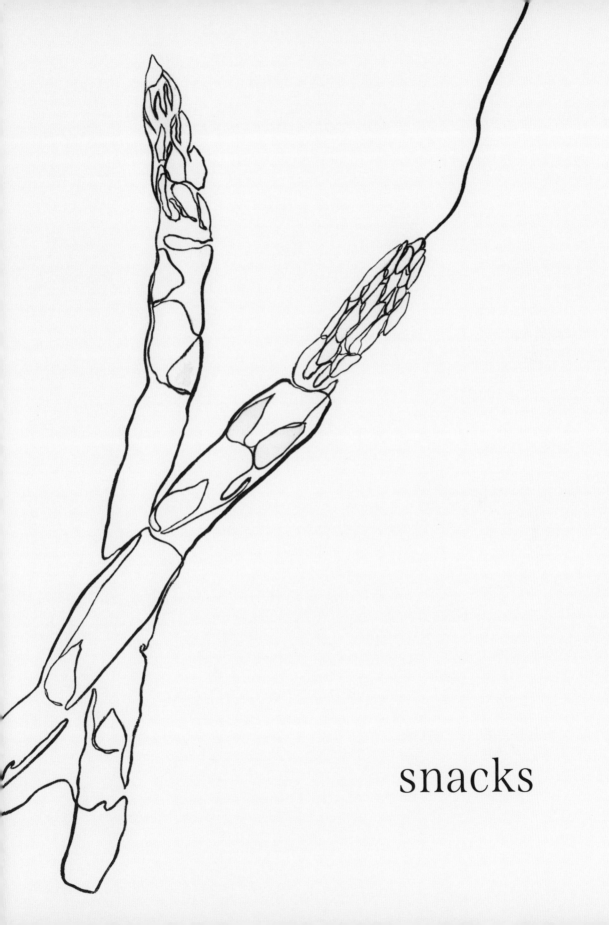

snacks

These delicious little vegetable snacks are simple to make and great all the year round. When frying be sure to have a selection of sizes as the little crispy parts are always the best. I have used regular flour here, but it will work just as well with gluten-free flour.

Vegetable bhajis
WITH CASHEW BUTTER & PICKLED ORANGE

MAKES 24

FOR THE CASHEW BUTTER
200g cashews

FOR THE PICKLED ORANGE
1 orange, peeled and segmented
pickle liquid (see page 258)
mint sprigs, to garnish

FOR THE BHAJIS
1 large cauliflower, leaves
    discarded and broken into florets
2 banana shallots, thinly
    sliced lengthways
4 spring onions, thinly sliced
2 carrots, peeled and grated
1 bunch of coriander,
    finely chopped
100g self-raising flour
220g plain flour
2 teaspoons cumin seeds
1 teaspoon chilli powder
½ teaspoon paprika
½ teaspoon ground coriander
2 teaspoons ground turmeric
2 teaspoons onion seeds
cooking oil, for frying
salt and freshly ground
    black pepper

Heat the oven to 180°C/160°C fan/Gas Mark 4. Tip the cashews into a baking tray and roast for 15 minutes, giving them a shake halfway through cooking, until golden brown. Allow to cool.

To make the cashew butter, blend the roasted cashews in a food processor, adding a small amount of water at a time until you have a smooth paste. Season to taste and keep in a plastic container or piping bag until needed. (You might need to scale up the recipe to give you a quantity that will blend until smooth. The extra butter will keep in an airtight container in the fridge for up to 5 days – it is delicious on toast or used as a dip.)

To pickle the orange, place the segments in a bowl or container and cover with pickle liquid. Set aside.

For the bhajis, using a mandolin slice the cauliflower florets into thin slices, making sure that no cauliflower goes to waste. Place the slices in a mixing bowl and add the shallots, spring onions and grated carrots. Season with salt and toss together well. Finally, add the chopped coriander.

Place both flours, all the spices and the onion seeds together in a separate bowl. Slowly whisk in 250ml of water to create a paste. Add this to the salted vegetables and use your hands to mix, making sure all the ingredients are coated in the paste.

Pour the cooking oil into a deep pan until two-thirds full and heat to 180°C on a cooking thermometer or until a cube of day-old bread turns golden in 60 seconds (or preheat a deep-fat fryer to 180°C).

Place a good spoonful of the bhaji mixture into the hot oil and cook for about 2 minutes on each side, until golden brown and crisp. Remove from the oil using a slotted spoon and set aside to drain on kitchen paper. Keep warm. Repeat for the remaining mixture, frying a few bhajis at a time, but taking care not to overcrowd the pan. Season the fritters after frying.

Serve with a spoonful of the cashew butter and the pickled orange and fresh mint sprinkled on top.

If you are lucky enough to be able to source very fresh vegetables from a local farm shop or farmers' market then this hummus dip is the perfect way to show them off. Simply give them a wash and make sure there is no dirt. You can use what vegetables you wish; I have chosen my favourites but please pick yours.

If you don't have lovely fresh vegetables to hand, then the hummus goes wonderfully with bread or crisps.

Cashew & chickpea hummus
WITH RAW VEGETABLES OR CRUDITÉS

SERVES 4

FOR THE CASHEW HUMMUS
350g cashew nuts, roasted
   (see page 22)
1 x 400g tin of chickpeas, drained,
   juice reserved
1 tablespoon tahini
1 roasted garlic bulb (see page
   267), flesh squeezed out
good squeeze of lemon juice
15ml sherry vinegar
60ml rapeseed oil
1 pinch of ground cumin
1 pinch of ground coriander
1 pinch of paprika
450ml chickpea juice topped
   up with water
onion powder, to serve
2 teaspoons rapeseed oil, to serve
salt and freshly ground
   black pepper

FOR THE VEGETABLE CRUDITÉS
1 bunch of radishes with tops
1 handful of sugar snap peas
1 bunch of baby carrots
2 heads of gem lettuce, leaves
   separated and torn if large
1 cauliflower, florets separated

You'll need a good-quality food processor to make really good hummus, although most standard kitchen versions will do the job well enough. Blend all the ingredients apart from the chickpea juice or water into a nice paste, then slowly add in the chickpea juice or water until the mixture is nice and smooth. Season with some salt and pepper along the way.

To serve, arrange the crudités nicely in a bowl. Transfer the hummus to a separate serving bowl, for dipping into. Finish with some onion powder and a sprinkling of rapeseed oil (although chilli oil, fresh herbs or nuts are all great finishes, too).

Forget fried chicken, this celeriac is all you will need to satisfy your KFC cravings. The sauce is easy to make and demands just a few specialist ingredients, though nothing you can't find in a large supermarket, and will help transform all sorts of dishes. It also keeps very well.

Buttermilk-fried celeriac
WITH KOREAN-STYLE SAUCE

SERVES 5

FOR THE SAUCE
150g gochujang paste
100ml dark soy sauce
50g light brown soft sugar
25ml mirin
75ml rice wine vinegar
2 garlic cloves
50ml sesame oil
50g stem ginger and
    1 tablespoon syrup

FOR THE FRIED CELERIAC
1 celeriac
1 litre cooking oil, for frying, plus 1
    teaspoon for rubbing the celeriac
200g buttermilk (or oat milk for a
    vegan version)
dredge (see page 263)
2 teaspoons chopped coriander
2 tablespoons sesame seeds,
    toasted (see page 230)
sea salt

For the sauce simply place all the ingredients into a food processor and blend until smooth. Add a little water if needed to reach a nice, saucy consistency. Keep in the fridge in a sealed container until needed.

Heat the oven to 200°C/180°C fan/Gas Mark 6.

Rub the celeriac with the teaspoon of oil and then rub over a good amount of sea salt and wrap the celeriac tightly in foil. Cover with a further 4 layers of foil – this helps the celeriac almost steam itself and leaves it with an amazing texture. Bake for about 1½ hours (the exact time will depend on the size of your celeriac), until tender when pierced with a sharp knife. Then, remove it from the oven and leave it to cool in the foil for 2 hours or so.

Remove the foil and then, using a knife, remove the celeriac skin, taking as little flesh away as possible. Using your hands, tear the celeriac flesh into small chunks – different sizes is best, so you end up with some nice, small crispy bits alongside some lovely large pieces.

Pour the cooking oil into a deep pan until two-thirds full and heat the oil to 180°C on a cooking thermometer or until a cube of day-old bread turns golden in 60 seconds (or preheat a deep-fat fryer to 180°C).

Get 2 mixing bowls: put the buttermilk (or oat milk) in one of them and the dredge in the other. Using your hands, place the celeriac pieces into the buttermilk or oat milk first, then into the dredge. Make sure the celeriac pieces have a good coating on them. Fry the pieces in batches, for about 3 minutes per batch, until golden and crisp. Set aside each batch to drain on kitchen paper, while you fry the next. Once all the pieces are fried and drained, place them in a clean mixing bowl, season them slightly with salt and coat them in the sauce. Finish with a sprinkling of chopped coriander and toasted sesame seeds.

We have a tradition of chef meals at Root and this brilliant dish was created one summer by the team. It's super tasty and can be paired with practically anything – spicy, sweet, crunchy, fresh and delicious. We use this gochujang dressing in any number of dishes, from grilled sardines to pork loin and beyond.

Gochujang is a spicy condiment made from fermented chilli that can be found online or in most supermarkets these days.

Gem & herb salad
WITH GOCHUJANG DRESSING

SERVES 4

FOR THE DRESSING
40g gochujang paste
20ml chardonnay vinegar
10g Dijon mustard
1 pinch of salt
200ml rapeseed oil
squeeze of lime juice, to taste

FOR THE GEM SALAD
100g raw peanuts
50g sesame seeds
1 red onion, thinly sliced
pickle liquid (see page
    258; optional)
2 baby gem heads, leaves
    separated
½ bunch of coriander, leaves
    picked, stalks finely chopped
½ bunch of mint, leaves picked
1 carrot, peeled and sliced into
    ribbons, or julienned
1 cucumber, sliced into ribbons,
    or julienned

To make the dressing, place the paste, vinegar, mustard and pinch of salt in a mixing bowl. Slowly whisk in the oil, making sure it emulsifies to create a thick, bright dressing. Whisk in the lime juice. If the dressing is too thick, add a splash of water to loosen. Set aside.

Heat the oven to 180°C/160°C fan/Gas Mark 4. On a tray spread out the peanuts and sesame seeds and toast in the oven for 10–15 minutes, giving them a shake halfway through cooking, until lightly coloured and aromatic. Remove from the oven and allow to cool, then use the back of a saucepan to roughly crush the nuts and seeds on the tray. Set aside.

Lightly pickling the red onion takes away some of its raw, bitter harshness. To do this, place the onions in a bowl and pour over a little pickle liquid. Leave them to steep until you have completed the salad. (If you don't have any pickle liquid to hand, unpickled raw red onion is still a great addition.)

Place the gem leaves into a large bowl. Add the coriander leaves and chopped coriander stalks, and the mint leaves. (You don't need the mint stalks for this salad – they are more fibrous than coriander stalks – but don't throw them away: use them in other cooking to add a minty flavour. For example, they are delicious over buttery, boiled new potatoes.)

Add the carrot and cucumber ribbons or slices. Finish with the crushed nuts and seeds and some drained pickled red onion (or red onion slices if you haven't pickled). Dress the salad liberally with the spicy dressing and toss well, making sure everything is well coated. Serve straight away in a beautiful salad bowl.

Salsify has a singular flavour and is extremely versatile and also very underrated. Known as the 'oyster plant' for its oyster-like flavour, it's a great pairing for seafood. In this recipe it is first cooked in oil, breadcrumbed and then fried, though you could also confit, steam or roast – all methods work very well.

Crispy salsify
WITH ROASTED GARLIC MAYONNAISE

SERVES 4

FOR THE GARLIC MAYONNAISE
3 egg yolks (about 60g)
30ml white wine vinegar
squeezed pulp of 2 roasted
   garlic bulbs (see page 267)
35g Dijon mustard
1 pinch of paprika
500ml cooking oil
squeeze of lemon juice
salt

FOR THE CRISPY SALSIFY
6 salsify roots
1 bay leaf
a few thyme sprigs
1 garlic clove, crushed
about 500ml cooking oil,
   plus extra for frying
100g plain flour
3 eggs, beaten
250g dried breadcrumbs
   (use panko, if possible)
100g Parmesan, grated
salt and freshly ground
   black pepper

First, make the garlic mayonnaise (the recipe will make more than you need – the remainder will keep in the fridge for 3–5 days). Put the yolks, vinegar, garlic, mustard and paprika in a bowl, season with salt and whisk together to combine. Using an electric whisk, slowly trickle in the oil, creating an emulsion. (You can do this in an electric mixer, if you prefer.) Whisk in the lemon juice and taste for seasoning. If the mayonnaise is too thick, add a little water to loosen to your preferred consistency. Set aside while you make the crispy salsify.

Heat the oven to 150°C/130°C fan/Gas Mark 2. Peel the salsify roots and put them straight into cold water. Drain off the water, top and tail the roots slightly and place them in a baking tray. Salt them well and leave them for 10 minutes to release a little moisture. Drain off the liquid from the roots, then add the bay, thyme and garlic. Cover with the cooking oil and place a piece of baking paper over the top of the baking tray and cook the salsify in the oven for 25 minutes, until just tender and so that it still holds its shape. Remove from the oven and leave to cool in the oil. When the salsify has cooled, remove from the oil and cut into about 2cm pieces.

Have 3 mixing bowls ready. Place the flour in the first bowl and the beaten eggs in the second. In the third, mix together the breadcrumbs and Parmesan. One by one, dip each salsify piece into the flour, then into the egg and finally into the cheesy breadcrumbs. Make sure the salsify pieces are well coated at each stage, gently shaking off any excess. Refrigerate the coated pieces until you're ready to cook (they will keep for about 1–2 days).

When you're ready, pour the cooking oil into a deep pan until two-thirds full and heat to 180°C on a cooking thermometer or until a cube of day-old bread turns golden in 60 seconds (or preheat a deep-fat fryer to 180°C).

Place the salsify in the fryer and cook until golden brown. Remove the pieces from the oil, drain on kitchen paper, then season with salt and some pepper, if you wish. (Alternatively, you can bake the coated salsify in the oven at 200°C/180°C fan/Gas Mark 6 for 15 minutes, until golden brown and crisp.) Serve the crispy salsify pieces while they're hot, alongside a good amount of mayonnaise for dipping.

These Japanese-style spring onions are one of our most popular snacks in the restaurant – they're rather like a deliciously elegant onion ring. The chilli sauce will keep well in the fridge and is handy to have around the kitchen for those times when you fancy a little bit of sweet heat. Vary the vegetables and if you want a bit more heat in the sauce add some extra dried chilli flakes.

Tempura spring onions
WITH SWEET CHILLI SAUCE & PEANUT CRUMB

SERVES 4

FOR THE SWEET CHILLI SAUCE
50g red chilli, halved, deseeded
   and finely sliced
50g fresh ginger root, peeled
   and finely sliced
2 garlic cloves, finely chopped
250g caster sugar
275ml white wine vinegar
20ml sesame oil
25ml lime juice
25ml dark soy sauce

FOR THE PEANUT CRUMB
200g raw peanuts
1 pinch of allspice
1 pinch of ground coriander
1 pinch of sea salt

FOR THE TEMPURA ONIONS
16 spring onions
cooking oil, for frying
140g plain flour
60g cornflour
1 teaspoon bicarbonate of soda
1 teaspoon baking powder
a few ice cubes
about 200ml sparkling water
burnt onion powder
   (see page 270), to serve
2 tablespoons chopped coriander
salt

For the chilli sauce, place the chilli, ginger and garlic in a metal container and keep to one side.

Place the sugar and white wine vinegar in a heavy-based saucepan and boil until the mixture reaches 113°C on a cooking thermometer – keep an eye on it as it won't take long. Pour the hot vinegar mixture over the chilli, ginger and garlic mixture and leave to cool. Once cool, add the sesame oil, lime juice and soy sauce and whisk well. If it thickens too much, add a little water until you reach your desired consistency.

Make the peanut crumb. Heat the oven to 180°C/160°C fan/Gas Mark 4. Spread the peanuts evenly over a baking tray and roast for 15–20 minutes, giving them a shake halfway through cooking, until golden brown. Remove from the oven and allow to cool.

Place the peanuts, spices and salt into a blender and blitz to a fine crumb – be careful not to over-blend as the mixture will turn into a paste very quickly.

For the tempura onions, bring a pan of salted water to the boil and have a bowl of iced water ready to go on the side.

Cook the onions in the boiling water for 1 minute, then remove them and immediately plunge them into the iced water.

Pour the cooking oil into a deep pan until two-thirds full and heat the oil to 180°C on a cooking thermometer or until a cube of day-old bread turns golden in 60 seconds (or preheat a deep-fat fryer to 180°C).

...method continued on page 34

To make the batter, mix together the flour, cornflour, bicarbonate of soda and baking powder in a bowl. Add the ice cubes (these keep the batter nice and cold) and slowly whisk in the sparkling water, a little at a time, until you have a batter that will just coat the onions. Working in batches, dip the onions in the batter, coating fully, but allowing some of the excess to drip off, so you don't over cover.

Place the onions in the hot oil for 2 minutes, or until crisp. Remove from the oil and drain well on kitchen paper, then sprinkle over a little onion powder and season with salt. Keep warm while you fry the remaining batches.

To serve, place a few of the onions on each plate. Drizzle with sweet chilli sauce, sprinkle with the peanut crumb and season with a further sprinkling of onion powder and a little chopped coriander. Serve a small bowl of sweet chilli sauce on the side, too, for dipping.

I developed these fantastic vegetable scotch eggs for my very first menu at Root. I wanted something delicious and simple and surprising – a dish usually associated with meat that everyone would enjoy and be amazed by, and that was also fun to make. The mix can also be used to make a brilliant vegetarian Kiev – simply use the mix to cover 25g of garlic butter and breadcrumb and you have yourself another wonderful meat-free meal.

Mushroom & lentil Scotch egg

MAKES 6

FOR THE LENTILS
300g puy lentils
1 litre homemade or good-quality
  vegetable stock
200ml red wine
a few rosemary or thyme
  sprigs (optional)
9 eggs
100g plain flour
250g dried breadcrumbs
  (use panko, if possible)
cooking oil, for frying
salt and freshly ground
  black pepper

FOR THE MUSHROOM DUXELLE
500g flat field mushrooms
3 tablespoons cooking oil
2 shallots, finely diced
1 garlic clove, minced
1 roasted garlic bulb (see page
  267), flesh squeezed out
1 thyme sprig, leaves picked
  and chopped
1 teaspoon cep powder (optional)
1 teaspoon truffle oil (optional)
1 teaspoon sherry vinegar
salt and freshly ground
  black pepper

Soak the lentils in a bowlful of water – overnight if you are very prepared, or for at least 1 hour is great, if not. Drain and rinse them off, then put them in a saucepan with the vegetable stock and red wine. Place the pan on a medium heat, season with salt and pepper and, if you do have some rosemary or thyme around, they are always good to add to the cooking liquid. Add the lentils, bring back to a simmer and cook for about 15–20 minutes, until soft.

While the lentils are cooking, bring a pan of salted water to the boil. Add 6 of the eggs and boil for just over 5 minutes, which should give you a good soft boil. Remove the eggs with a slotted spoon and plunge them straight into iced water to get a nice runny yolk.

When the lentils are soft, drain them, then spread them out over a large plate to allow them to cool and dry evenly (you don't want the mixture to be too wet as you need it to mould around the egg). Put the cooled lentils into a food processor and blend to create a thick paste, then set aside.

For the duxelle, either hand chop or pulse the mushrooms in a food processor, to give you a mushroom crumb. Heat the cooking oil in a saucepan over a medium heat and add the shallots and the minced and roasted garlic. Sweat them down for about 3–4 minutes, until slightly soft, then add the chopped thyme, followed by the blitzed mushrooms. On a low heat, season with a good amount of salt and pepper and add the cep powder (if using).

Cook the duxelle on a low heat for about 15–20 minutes, until the mixture has released all its water content and is nice and dry and you are left with a nice pâté (duxelle).

...method continued on page 36

Mix together the duxelle and lentil purée in a bowl and season with salt and pepper. I like to add a touch of truffle oil and a little sherry vinegar. This is what you'll be using as the 'sausagemeat' for your Scotch eggs. Place the mixture in the fridge for a few minutes to set a bit to make it easier to mould it around the eggs.

Crack the remaining 3 eggs into a bowl and beat lightly with a fork. Place the flour in a second bowl and the breadcrumbs in a third. Then, peel the boiled eggs, ready to coat them.

Weigh out 100g of the lentil and mushroom mixture and flatten it out into a thin patty in your hand. Place 1 boiled egg in the centre of the patty and carefully mould the mixture around the egg. Dip each coated egg into the flour, then into the beaten egg and finally into the breadcrumbs, coating well at each stage and gently shaking off any excess. Set aside on a plate and repeat for the remaining eggs and mixture. Refrigerate the coated eggs until you're ready to cook.

Preheat the oven to 200°C/180°C fan/Gas Mark 6.

Pour the cooking oil into a deep pan until two-thirds full and heat to 180°C on a thermometer or until a cube of day-old bread turns golden in 60 seconds (or preheat a deep-fat fryer to 180°C).

Gently place each Scotch egg into the hot oil and cook for about 4 minutes, until golden brown, then transfer the egg to the oven for 2 minutes to really warm it through. Repeat for all the eggs.

Serve warm with your preferred sauces – for me it has to be with ketchup or a decent brown sauce. See pages 42–43 for our own brown sauce recipe.

Like many, I love fresh sweetcorn in the husk when in season. This is an upgraded version of the classic grilled sweetcorn with butter and a little salt – when you have a great ingredient the simple treatment is often best.

The spiced butter is great not only with sweetcorn but also with many other dishes so make a large batch and freeze it or keep it in the fridge, using it perhaps for roasting vegetables, meat or fish, or to finish dishes such as risotto.

Grilled sweetcorn
WITH HONEY & SPICED BUTTER

SERVES 4

4 corn-on-the-cobs, in their husks
2–4 tablespoons rapeseed oil
4 tablespoons runny honey
sea salt

FOR THE SPICED BUTTER
250g unsalted butter
2 teaspoons paprika
1 teaspoon ground white pepper
1 teaspoon garlic powder
1 teaspoon onion powder
1 teaspoon salt
1 teaspoon sherry vinegar
1 teaspoon tomato purée
1 teaspoon Worcestershire sauce
1 teaspoon cumin
1 teaspoon ground coriander
1 teaspoon Tabasco sauce

First, make the spiced butter. Simply soften the butter and put it in the bowl of a stand mixer. Add all the other ingredients and mix, using the whisk or a paddle attachment, until combined. Alternatively, if you're like me, you can do this in a bowl using your hands. (You'll have more spiced butter than you need for this recipe, but it will keep in a container in the fridge for 3–5 days and you can use it for roasting vegetables, meat or fish, or for finishing off a risotto – among many other things.)

Bring a large saucepan of salted water to the boil. Discard the corn husks and boil the corns for 5–6 minutes, depending on size, until the kernels are tender.

Get a griddle or grill nice and hot – or, of course, a barbecue is even better.

Rub the cobs in a little of the rapeseed oil and place them on the grill. Cook on each side for about 1–2 minutes, until you have a nice char and smoky flavour. Using a pastry brush, spread the spiced butter nicely over the corns while they're still on the grill. When the corns are ready, remove them from the grill and top each with another knob of the butter, if you think they need it. Allow the butter to melt, then drizzle each corn with a spoonful of honey and sprinkle with a pinch of sea salt. Serve straight away.

These are quite simply the most adult cheesy chips ever! They are great just on their own or alongside a main dish. I would recommend making the terrine the day before as it needs time to press and set. You will need a terrine mould or a loaf tin.

Crispy potato & cheese terrine

MAKES 1 TERRINE/SERVES 6–8

200g unsalted butter
150g strong Cheddar, grated
12–15 large Maris Piper potatoes,
    peeled and cut into 2–3mm
    slices (don't put the slices
    in water)
cooking oil, for frying
100g Parmesan, finely grated,
    to serve
salt and freshly ground
    black pepper

Heat the oven to 180°C/160°C fan/Gas Mark 4. Line a terrine mould with baking paper. Leave enough height and overlap in the paper so that you can fold it over the top to cover when cooking the terrine, and just to make sure there are no difficulties when you need to remove the terrine from the tin. You want to have everything ready so it is as simple as slicing and building.

Melt the butter in a saucepan over a low heat. Remove from the heat and keep the butter next to you, along with a pastry brush, the salt and pepper, and the grated cheese.

Start layering the potatoes in the mould, slightly overlapping each slice. Brush each layer with butter, then season it with salt and pepper before beginning the next. Once you're a third of the way up the mould, add a layer of grated Cheddar (use about one-third of the Cheddar). Continue with the buttered and seasoned potato layers until you're two-thirds of the way up, and add another layer of Cheddar. Keep building until you are a couple of layers above the mould lip – the terrine will shrink and compress when cooking. Finish with a final layer of grated Cheddar.

Fold the baking paper over the top of the layers and cover with foil. Bake for 1 hour 35 minutes, until you are able to push a skewer or knife through the layers without much resistance and the top is a lovely golden colour. If not, remove the foil and cook the terrine, uncovered, for a further 10 minutes.

Remove the terrine from the oven and put it on a baking tray to catch any buttery drips that might spill over when you press it down (you don't want this all over your fridge). Find something that fits well in the mould to press down with – maybe another mould or loaf tin. Position the press on top and give it a good push downwards. Then, weigh down the press with something – maybe a few tins of food. Set aside to cool in the fridge.

When the terrine is cold, pour the cooking oil into a deep pan until two-thirds full and heat to 180°C on a cooking thermometer or until a cube of day-old bread turns golden in 60 seconds (or preheat a deep-fat fryer to 180°C). Remove the terrine from the tin and slice it into whatever shapes you wish – we have gone for chip-like pieces. Deep fry the pieces for about 2 minutes, until golden and crisp all over (you can pan fry in a good amount of oil, if you prefer, making sure the pieces are golden on all sides). Serve immediately sprinkled with a good amount of grated Parmesan.

My number one go-to snack of all time is cheese and Branston pickle, so when I created these arancini and served them up with brown sauce they tasted just like the best cheese and pickle – but even better!

Cheese & onion arancini
WITH BROWN SAUCE

MAKES 24

FOR THE ARANCINI
3 tablespoons cooking oil,
 plus 1 litre for frying
2 shallots, diced
1 roasted garlic bulb (see page
 267), flesh squeezed out
1 garlic clove, chopped
200g risotto rice
1 teaspoon smoked paprika
250g white wine
800ml hot vegetable stock
300g burnt onion purée
 (see page 267)
250g Cheddar, grated
50g unsalted butter
1 teaspoon sherry vinegar
1 teaspoon lemon juice
1 teaspoon Worcestershire sauce
splash of Tabasco sauce
100g plain flour
3 eggs, beaten
250g dried breadcrumbs (use
 panko if possible)
100g Gouda cheese, grated,
 to serve
salt and freshly ground
 black pepper

For the arancini, heat the 3 tablespoons of oil in a large saucepan on a medium heat. Add the shallots, roasted garlic and chopped garlic and sweat for 1 minute, stirring well. Add the risotto rice and paprika and keep stirring – you may need to add a little more oil if the pan becomes too dry. Cook for a further 1 minute, then add the white wine and stir to deglaze the bottom of the pan.

Add the first ladleful of stock and cook, stirring, until the rice has absorbed the liquid. Continue ladling in the stock, little by little, stirring all the time and making sure the stock is absorbed before adding the next ladleful. Simmer until the rice is softened, then add the onion purée, Cheddar and butter and cook until the rice is completely tender and the butter and cheese have melted. The whole process will take about 25 minutes.

Season the risotto with salt and pepper, then add the sherry vinegar, lemon juice, Worcestershire sauce and Tabasco. Transfer the mixture to a baking tray and leave to cool before placing in the fridge to chill and set hard.

While the rice is chilling, make the brown sauce. Place the apples, prunes and onion in a saucepan and cover with water. Place over a high heat and bring to the boil, then boil for about 5–10 minutes, until soft. Strain the mixture through a sieve, place it in a food processor with the malt vinegar and blend until you have a smooth purée.

Transfer the purée to a clean saucepan with the balsamic vinegar and all the remaining sauce ingredients. Place the pan on a low heat and cook, whisking from time to time, until the sauce has reduced to a ketchup-like consistency (about 10–15 minutes). Transfer the sauce back into the food processor and blend again until completely smooth. Cool, transfer to a suitable container and store in the fridge until needed. (You will have more brown sauce than you need for this recipe – but it lasts up to 6 months in the fridge and is delicious on just about anything.)

FOR THE BROWN SAUCE

400g eating apples (such as
Granny Smith), peeled,
cored and sliced
120g pitted prunes
1 onion, sliced
180ml malt vinegar
180ml balsamic vinegar
220g caster sugar
1 pinch of ground ginger
1 pinch of ground nutmeg
1 pinch of allspice
1 pinch of cayenne pepper
1 teaspoon salt

Roll the chilled risotto into 50g balls (you should get about 24 balls altogether), replacing them on the tray and putting them back in the fridge to firm up again (you could freeze the balls at this point, if you like, then continue with the method when you're ready to cook, using the frozen balls).

Gather 3 mixing bowls. Place the flour in the first bowl, the beaten egg in the second and the breadcrumbs in the third. One by one, dip the arancini into the flour, then into the beaten egg and finally into the breadcrumbs. Make sure the balls are well coated at each stage, gently shaking off any excess. Refrigerate until you're ready to cook and serve.

Pour the cooking oil into a deep pan until two-thirds full and heat to 180°C on a cooking thermometer or until a cube of day-old bread turns golden in 60 seconds (or preheat a deep-fat fryer to 180°C).

Working in batches of 5 or 6 arancini at a time, place the arancini into the oil and cook for 2–3 minutes, until golden brown. Set each batch aside to drain on kitchen paper and keep warm while you fry the remainder. Serve immediately with the brown sauce on the side and plenty of grated Gouda on top.

It's rare to see hasselback potatoes on menus anymore which is a great shame – they are seen as being a bit old school. One day our friend Nicholas Balfe from Salon and Levan came and cooked with us at Root. He magicked up these Hasselback Jerusalem artichokes, and they blew us away. From then on we hasselbacked everything and this was our favourite: not so old-school anymore and great as a snack or a side dish.

Hasselback parsnips
WITH HONEY-MUSTARD MAYONNAISE

SERVES 4

FOR THE MAYONNAISE
3 egg yolks (about 60g)
30ml white wine vinegar
1 pinch of salt
35g Dijon mustard
30g wholegrain mustard
2 tablespoons runny honey
500ml cooking oil
squeeze of lemon juice

FOR THE HASSELBACK PARSNIPS
6 parsnips, peeled and cut in half
    lengthways
cooking oil, for frying or roasting
2 tablespoons chopped chives
salt

First, make the mayonnaise (the recipe will make more than you need, but the remainder will keep in the fridge for 3–5 days). In a bowl, whisk together the yolks, vinegar, salt, both mustards and the honey. For ease, ask someone to hold the bowl for you and then, using an electric whisk, slowly trickle in the oil, creating an emulsion. (You can do this in an electric mixer, if you prefer.) When you have added all the oil, you will have a mayonnaise. Finally, whisk in the lemon juice and taste for seasoning. If the mayonnaise is too thick, add a little water to loosen to your preferred consistency. Set aside while you make the parsnips.

At the restaurant, we use the fryer to make these and this gives the best flavour and colour, but they are very much achievable in an oven. If you're using a fryer, set it to 125°C; if you're using an oven, heat it to 220°C/200°C fan/Gas Mark 7.

With the cut sides of the parsnip halves downwards and using a sharp knife, score deeply across the width of each parsnip at 1.5mm intervals, all the way along the length – you don't want to slice all the way through, just make deep cuts, leaving the base intact.

If you're deep-frying, fry the scored parsnips for 4–5 minutes, until softened. If you're using an oven, bring a pan of salted water to the boil and blanch the parsnips for 4–5 minutes. Using a slotted spoon, remove them from the fryer or pan and set aside to drain on kitchen paper.

Then, if frying: turn up the fryer to 180°C and, working in batches, fry the hasselbacks for 2–3 minutes, until golden. Set each batch aside to drain on kitchen paper and keep warm while you fry the remainder. If baking: rub the parsnips with a little oil, then place them in a roasting tin. Bake in the hot oven for 10–12 minutes, until golden.

Place the cooked hassleback parsnips in a bowl, season with chives and salt and serve immediately with the mayonnaise alongside.

Old-school salad cream is fantastic, easy to make and one of those evocative taste memories that takes me straight back to my childhood. And when matched with these fantastic polenta chips it becomes something very special. I make the salad cream with plain flour, but it will work just as well with gluten-free flour.

Polenta chips
& SALAD CREAM

SERVES 4

FOR THE POLENTA CHIPS
1 litre whole milk
1 onion, halved
1 bay leaf
1 thyme sprig
3–5 black peppercorns
1 garlic clove, crushed
225g polenta, plus 80g for dusting
1 teaspoon truffle oil
1 pinch of paprika
1 pinch of onion powder
50g Parmesan, grated, plus
    optional extra to serve
rapeseed oil, for brushing
salt and freshly ground
    black pepper

FOR THE SALAD CREAM
1 tablespoon gluten-free
    or plain flour
3 tablespoons caster sugar
1 tablespoon mustard powder
100ml cider vinegar, or chardonnay
    or other good-quality white
    wine vinegar
2 eggs
150ml double cream
generous squeeze of lemon juice
a pinch of salt

Grease and line a 20cm (or near enough) square baking tin.

First, make the polenta. Place the milk in a saucepan and add the onion halves, bay, thyme, peppercorns and garlic. Bring to the boil over a medium heat, then turn off the heat and leave the milk to cool. Strain through a sieve into a jug and discard the contents of the sieve.

Place the infused milk in a saucepan over a medium heat. Bring to a simmer, then slowly whisk in the polenta until well incorporated. Season with salt and pepper, then add the truffle oil, paprika, onion powder and Parmesan. Reduce the heat to medium–low and continue stirring. Cook until the mixture has thickened well and the polenta has broken down and created a smooth mixture (about 12–15 minutes). Pour the polenta into the prepared tin, cool and refrigerate for about 1 hour to set.

Meanwhile, make the salad cream. Place a heatproof bowl over a pan of simmering water (use a low–medium heat), ensuring the bottom of the bowl doesn't touch the water, to create a bain marie. Put the flour, sugar, mustard powder and vinegar into the bowl. Crack in the eggs and stir to combine, then whisk until you have a very thick mixture – it should take 4–5 minutes and a good amount of whisking. Remove the bowl from the saucepan and leave the mixture to cool, then refrigerate. Once the mixture is fully chilled, stir in the cream, lemon juice and a pinch of salt, and a little water to loosen, if necessary (aim for your ideal consistency). You should have a very familiar-tasting salad cream.

Preheat the oven to 220°C/200°C fan/Gas Mark 7. Remove the set polenta from the tin on to a chopping board and cut it into chip-sized pieces (I prefer them on the smaller side as they go crispier). Dust using the 80g of polenta. Arrange the chips on a baking tray lined with baking paper and bake for about 30 minutes, until lovely and crisp.

To serve, place the polenta chips on a plate and scatter over some more grated Parmesan if you wish. Serve with the salad cream on the side, or (as I like it) drizzled all over the chips.

This is a lovely warm salad to have for lunch or dinner, or even as a side to a barbecue. You need a nice large gem that can handle the grilling and still retain a good crunch. And delicious as the grilled gem is, it's the seaweed mayonnaise that takes star billing and earns a standing ovation here.

Grilled gem
WITH SEAWEED MAYONNAISE & WALNUT SALSA

SERVES 4

FOR THE PICKLED SHALLOTS
2 shallots, cut into 2mm slices
pickle liquid (see page 258)
salt

FOR THE WALNUT SALSA
100g walnut halves
1 shallot, diced
1 teaspoon sherry vinegar
1 tablespoon rapeseed oil

FOR THE SEAWEED MAYONNAISE
3 egg yolks (about 60g)
30ml chardonnay or other good-
    quality white wine vinegar
35g Dijon mustard
1 pinch of dried seaweed flakes
500ml seaweed oil (see page 268)
squeeze of lemon juice
salt

FOR THE GRILLED GEM
4 large gem lettuces, split apart
cooking oil, for grilling
1 bunch of radishes, thinly sliced
salt and freshly ground black
    pepper

First, get the pickled shallots done. Place the shallot slices in a bowl and sprinkle with some salt. Pour over the pickling liquid to cover and leave while you make the rest of the recipe.

Heat the oven to 180°C/160°C fan/Gas Mark 4.

Make the walnut salsa. Roughly chop the walnuts and scatter them out over a baking tray. Place them in the oven and bake for 10 minutes, until toasted. Add the shallot, sherry vinegar and oil to the tray and give everything a mix. Return to the oven for a further 5 minutes, then remove from the oven and allow to cool. Set aside until needed.

Make the seaweed mayonnaise (the recipe will make more than you need, but the remainder will keep in the fridge for 3–5 days). Put the yolks, vinegar and mustard in a bowl, season with salt, add the seaweed flakes and whisk together to combine. For ease, ask someone to hold the bowl for you and then, using an electric whisk to mix with one hand, slowly trickle in the oil with the other, creating an emulsion. (You can do this in an electric mixer, if you prefer.) When you have added all the oil, you will have a lovely, bright green mayonnaise. Whisk in the lemon juice and taste for seasoning. If the mayonnaise is too thick, add a little water to loosen to your preferred consistency. Set aside.

Using a hot griddle, grill, barbecue or frying pan, brush the gem lettuce leaves with oil and season with salt and pepper, then place them face down on the grill (or equivalent). Leave to cook for 2 minutes, so that they become nicely charred, then turn them over and cook for a further 1 minute to char the other sides. Remove from the grill and transfer to a serving plate. Scatter the pickled shallots and walnut salsa over the top, drizzle over some seaweed mayonnaise and finish with lashings of sliced radish.

The Isle of Wight is renowned for its amazing tomatoes but, unknown to many, the island also produces wonderful crops of padrón peppers. Padrón are usually mild but a few can surprise with a heat kick to rattle the culinary senses. They are a great start to a summer's meal, ideally charred on a barbecue to a good blister, with the addition of a generous amount of sea salt to finish. The hung yoghurt and burnt onion powder are a perfect accompaniment to the gently threatening padróns.

Grilled Isle of Wight padrón peppers
WITH HUNG YOGHURT & BURNT ONION POWDER

MAKES 4

1 teaspoon sea salt, plus
   extra to season
200g natural yoghurt
400g Isle of Wight or other
   padrón peppers
about 60ml first-press rapeseed oil
2 teaspoons burnt onion powder
   (see page 270), for dusting

Line a sieve with a J-cloth and place the sieve over a container or mixing bowl. Stir the salt into the yoghurt then pour or spoon the mixture into the lined sieve. The yoghurt will thicken as the whey drips from it – after 30 minutes, spoon the thickened yoghurt out of the sieve into an airtight container. Refrigerate until you're ready to serve (it will keep well for 3–5 days).

In a large bowl dress the padrón pepper with the rapeseed oil and a good amount of salt. Heat a large frying pan on a high heat. Once you have a good amount of heat in the pan, add the peppers – don't overfill the pan (cook in 2 batches, if necessary). Cook the peppers on one side for 1 minute, or until the skins start to blister. Make sure the pan remains on a high heat and toss the peppers as they cook. Keep cooking for a further 2–3 minutes, until the peppers have softened and coloured all over. Remove from the pan and taste to check the seasoning.

Serve immediately with a dusting of burnt onion powder and a good helping of yoghurt on the side.

Less is more and the less you do to a good vegetable the better – and a Jerusalem artichoke is a good vegetable. The key to success is to grill the artichokes long enough and hot enough to caramelise and bring out their fantastic flavour.

Chargrilled Jerusalem artichokes
WITH GREEN SAUCE & CANDIED WALNUTS

SERVES 4

16 Jerusalem artichokes
salad dressing (see page 259)
3 tablespoons first-press
    rapeseed oil
artichoke crisps (see page
    94, optional)

FOR THE CANDIED WALNUTS
cooking oil, for frying
200g caster sugar
100g walnut halves
a pinch of salt

FOR THE GREEN SAUCE
1 shallot, sliced
1 bunch of coriander
12 mint sprigs, leaves picked
12 parsley sprigs
12 jalapeño slices, from a jar
50ml chardonnay or other good-
    quality white wine vinegar
250ml cooking oil
salt and freshly ground black
    pepper, to taste

Make sure the artichokes are washed well – their shape means they can carry a good amount of dirt. Bring the water of your steamer to the boil and place the artichokes in the steamer. Steam for anything from 20–45 minutes, depending on the variety, until softened. If you don't have a steamer, simmer in some slightly salted water until soft, then drain and pat dry.

While the artichokes are steaming, make the candied walnuts and the green sauce. For the candied walnuts, pour the cooking oil into a deep pan until two-thirds full and heat to 180°C on a cooking thermometer, or until a cube of day-old bread turns golden in 60 seconds (or preheat a deep-fat fryer to 180°C).

While the oil is heating, pour 200ml of water into a saucepan and add the sugar. Place over a medium heat and bring to a simmer, then add the walnuts. Using a cooking or sugar thermometer, bring the water temperature to 108°C, then remove the pan from the heat and drain the walnuts. Place the drained walnuts into the hot oil and deep fry for about 90 seconds, until golden brown. Remove from the oil using a slotted spoon and allow to drain well, then transfer them to a baking tray lined with a J-cloth. Season with the pinch of salt. Set aside.

For the green sauce, place all the ingredients into a food processor and blend for 1 minute, until you have a paste. Check the seasoning, then set aside until needed. (You can make this in advance, if you prefer – the sauce will keep in an airtight container in the fridge for up to 5 days, although it will discolour slightly after 48 hours.)

Warm a griddle or grill pan until hot. Halve the steamed artichokes and place them in a mixing bowl. Toss them with a little dressing, the 3 tablespoons of rapeseed oil and a little seasoning of salt and pepper, then place them on the grill or griddle. Cook for 4–5 minutes on each side, until charred and cooked through.

To serve, pour the green sauce over a plate, then top with the grilled artichokes. Scatter over the candied walnuts, and then the artichoke crisps, if you have them.

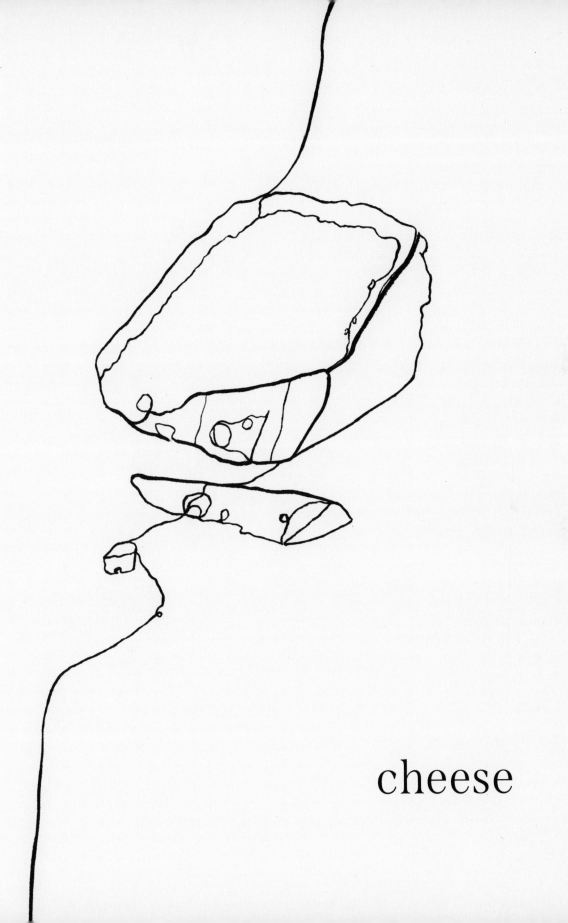

cheese

Think cheese on toast turned right up to 11. This recipe has featured on our menu on and off since the very first day. If it's not on the menu we get complaints! So, if you're looking for pure indulgence then look no further than this British classic. We use Westcombe Cheddar for its strong tangy flavour.

Lager rarebit
ON TOASTED SOURDOUGH

MAKES 4

150ml lager
100ml double cream
30ml Worcestershire sauce
25ml cider vinegar
pinch of paprika
pinch of mustard powder
250g good-quality Cheddar, grated
4 slices of sourdough bread

Heat the oven to 200°C/180°C fan/Gas Mark 6.

Put the lager, cream, Worcestershire sauce, vinegar, paprika and mustard powder in a large saucepan on a medium heat. Boil the mixture for 8–10 minutes, stirring occasionally, until it has reduced by three-quarters and is thicker and darker. Add the cheese and lower the heat. Cook for 4–5 minutes, until the cheese has melted and incorporated well.

Transfer the mixture to a food processor and blend until smooth and glossy. Add a little extra cream or some water to thin the mixture until you have a nice, spreadable consistency.

Allow the mixture to cool and lightly toast the sourdough. Spread a nice amount of rarebit on each piece of toast (use as much as you like and keep any remainder in the fridge for 3–5 days – but I'm sure it won't last that long; if you do chill the mixture, heat and re-blend before using), then transfer the toasts to a baking sheet and bake in oven for 4–5 minutes, until the topping is hot through and golden brown. (Finish the rarebit under a hot grill for 1 minute, if the top isn't quite lovely and golden after baking.)

Though sounding very fancy, a gougère is simply a savoury choux pastry made with cheese. And they are sublimely delicious. Once you have the technique perfected, they will become a firm favourite. They are great filled with almost anything and are at their best served warm straight from the oven with drinks or at the start of a meal, or for just general grazing.

Comté gougères

MAKES ABOUT 50

180g unsalted butter, cut into
    1cm dice
1 tablespoon salt, plus 1 pinch
250g plain flour
120g comté cheese, grated
pinch of freshly grated nutmeg
pinch of cayenne pepper
5 eggs
1 egg yolk
2 teaspoons paprika

Heat the oven to 200°C/180°C fan/Gas Mark 6. Boil 400ml of water in a medium–large saucepan. Add the butter and pinch of salt and leave to boil for 30 seconds before removing from the heat and adding the flour. Using a wooden spoon, beat the mixture together until it's fully blended and the dough is coming away from the sides of the pan. Put the dough in an electric stand mixer, if you have one, and, using the paddle attachment, mix for 1–2 minutes on medium speed, until the mixture is slightly cool.

Add the cheese, nutmeg and cayenne and mix again. The cheese will start to melt a little – although not fully – which is fine.

Add the eggs one at a time and the yolk, mixing continuously. Be patient: it might take a little work, but the eggs should incorporate nicely to leave you with a glossy, pipe-able mixture.

Line a baking tray with a silicone mat or a piece of baking paper. Use a little of the mixture to stick the paper to the tray, if necessary.

Spoon the mixture into a large piping bag fitted with a large, plain nozzle and pipe balls about 3cm in diameter over the lined baking sheet. Make them evenly sized so that they cook at the same rate and space them well apart to allow them to expand during cooking. (If you don't have a piping bag, submerge 2 dessert spoons in hot water to heat them up, then spoon the mixture out on to the baking tray as best you can to resemble balls.)

Try to avoid little pointed hats in your piped gougères, as these will burn during cooking. If you get them, dip a spoon in hot water and use the back of it to ever-so-slightly push them down.

Mix the paprika with the tablespoon of salt and sift the mixture over the gougères – give them a dusting, but not too much, as the flavour is intense.

Bake the gougères for 15–18 minutes, until the balls are beautifully golden. Enjoy hot out of the oven.

Chicory is an acquired taste but here its sometimes challenging bitterness marries perfectly with the sweet creamy cheese and fresh crisp apple to make a wonderful and versatile salad. Serve it as a canapé, a small palate-enlivening starter, a light lunch or as a delicious side to a main dish. In this version I've filled the leaves to make into tasty little bites.

Ewe's curd, turnip & apple-filled chicory leaves

SERVES 4

200g ewe's curd
zest and juice of ½ unwaxed lemon
2 tablespoons chopped chives
2 heads of chicory
1 turnip, peeled and diced
1 Granny Smith apple, cored
    and diced
1 mint sprig, leaves picked
salad dressing (see page 259)
    or 50ml first-press rapeseed
    oil, to taste
onion powder and parsley powder
    (optional), to serve
salt and freshly ground black
    pepper, plus extra salt for
    the turnip

FOR THE CROUTONS
¼ loaf of stale bread, cut into
    1cm pieces (remove the
    crust if it's very crunchy,
    such as sourdough)
1 thyme sprig
1 garlic clove, crushed
3 tablespoons rapeseed oil

Preheat the oven to 190°C/170°C fan/Gas Mark 5.

Put the ewe's curd, lemon zest and juice and chives in a bowl. Season with salt and pepper and mix well. Transfer to an airtight container and store in the fridge while you make the rest of the dish.

Make the croutons. Put the bread pieces into a baking tray with the thyme sprig and garlic. Sprinkle over the oil and season with salt and pepper. Make sure the croutons are nicely coated.

Cook in the oven for 10–15 minutes, giving them a shake halfway through, until golden brown. Remove from the oven and set aside to cool.

Prepare the chicory by cutting 5cm off the bottom of each chicory head and removing the leaves – they should come off whole. Keep cutting off the bottom after every few leaves until you're left with the little core. Reserve the leaves and discard the cores.

Place the diced turnip in a sieve and sprinkle over a pinch of salt. Leave for 10 minutes, then rinse in cold running water. Place the rinsed turnip into a bowl, add the diced apple, mint leaves, and a little dressing or the first-press rapeseed oil to taste.

Remove the ewe's curd mixture from the fridge 10 minutes before you intend to construct the dish. To serve, lightly dress the chicory leaves with some more of the dressing or rapeseed oil. Spoon a little of the ewe's curd mixture into each of the lightly dressed chicory leaves, spreading it out using the back of a spoon. Add spoonfuls of the turnip and apple mixture on to the curd and top with the croutons. You can finish with some onion powder or parsley powder to give everything a bit more colour and a little hit of flavour, if you wish.

If you want to achieve a 'wow' moment at a dinner party, then I would recommend producing this amazing dish. It has been on and off the menu at Root since we first opened. There is something magical about burrata – the fact that it's cheese wrapped in cheese might explain it! It's a perfect dish for sharing on a summer's evening with fresh tomatoes and grilled sourdough. You will be able to find a good-quality burrata at a local cheesemonger – ours comes from Rosie at the amazing The Bristol Cheesemonger on Wapping Wharf, just around the corner from Root.

Burrata
WITH MARINATED COURGETTES & PISTACHIO DUKKAH

SERVES 4

1 courgette, cut into 3mm slices
1 garlic clove, thinly sliced
25ml chardonnay or other good-
   quality white wine vinegar
100ml first-press rapeseed oil,
   plus extra to serve
2 burrata (about 100g each)
2 tablespoons aged
   balsamic vinegar
salt and freshly ground
   black pepper

FOR THE PISTACHIO DUKKAH
200g shelled pistachios
50g pumpkin seeds (optional)
50g sunflower seeds (optional)
10g cumin seeds
10g coriander seeds
20g sesame seeds

Preheat the oven to 180°C/160°C fan/Gas Mark 4. Put the courgettes and garlic into a container and lightly sprinkle them with salt. Pour the vinegar and oil over the courgettes and leave them to marinate for about 5 minutes. Transfer the courgettes to a bowl and set aside. (Or, make in advance and transfer them to an airtight container and keep them in the fridge for 2–3 days.)

To make the dukkah, scatter the pistachios and the pumpkin and sunflower seeds, if using, over a baking tray. Roast in the oven for 12–15 minutes, until toasted. Place the cumin and coriander seeds on a second tray and the sesame seeds on a third tray. Roast these for 10 minutes, until toasted.

Slightly blend the cumin and coriander seeds to break them up a little to a coarse texture, but not so much that they are ground. Keep the sesame seeds whole and set aside a handful of pumpkin and sunflower seeds (if using) and a handful of the pistachio nuts.

Pulse the remaining nuts and seeds in a spice grinder, or, if you don't have a spice grinder, wrap them in a tea towel and use a saucepan to bash them up to a fine texture.

In a bowl, mix together all the nuts and seeds in their various guises for a great-looking dukkah. Season with a pinch of black pepper and sea salt. (The recipe will make more dukkah than you need, but it will keep in an airtight container in a dry place for up to 4 weeks. Use it to add crunch and flavour to salads or sides, for example.)

Just before you're ready to serve, first remove the burrata from the fridge for 15–20 minutes to let them come up to room temperature.

Drain the liquid from the burrata and place it in the centre of a nice plate or bowl. Season with salt and pepper and drizzle with a little more oil. Drizzle the balsamic vinegar around the outside and sprinkle with the dukkah. Place the sliced courgettes on and around the burrata to finish.

A chefs' trip to Dorset was the inspiration for this wonderful fruit loaf. We had set off to buy some cheeses from a great local cheesemonger and there, sitting on the counter when we entered, was a glorious freshly baked fruit loaf. The cheesemonger told us we had to try it toasted with the soft cheese we'd bought and from that came the inspiration for this lovely combination of flavour and texture.

The loaf is amazing with or without the cheese, but it always demands plenty of butter. It also freezes well in carefully cut slices, perfect for popping in the toaster when peckish.

Toasted fruit loaf
SERVED WITH TUNWORTH CHEESE

MAKES 1 LOAF

60g sultanas
60g golden raisins
2 Earl Grey tea bags
boiling water, from a kettle
480g strong white bread flour
15g fresh yeast
220ml whole milk
10g salt
60g caster sugar
100g unsalted butter, softened
2 eggs
2 egg yolks
60g dried apricots, finely chopped

FOR THE EGG WASH
1 egg
1 tablespoon milk

TO SERVE
salted butter, for toasting
300g Tunworth cheese, or an
    alternative such as brie, cut
    into slices

Place the sultanas and golden raisins with the 2 tea bags in a bowl. Pour over boiling water until the fruit and tea bags are just covered and steep for at least 30 minutes.

Meanwhile, lightly grease a 900g loaf tin and heat the oven to 200°C/180°C fan/Gas Mark 6.

Put the flour and yeast in the bowl of a stand mixer fitted with the dough hook. Mix the two together on a low speed for about 5 minutes.

Halfway through mixing, in a small saucepan, heat the milk over a low heat for about 2 minutes, until lukewarm. Set aside until needed (the heat will help the dough when it's rising).

Add the salt, sugar and softened butter to the bowl with the flour and yeast and mix on medium speed for about 5 minutes, until the butter is incorporated. Crack in the eggs and add the egg yolks, then add the warmed milk and continue mixing on medium speed for a further 8–10 minutes, until the dough comes together.

While the dough is mixing, drain the sultanas and raisins, discarding any tea left in the bowl, and combine the fruit in a bowl with the chopped apricots.

Once the dough has come together, turn the mixer to a low speed and continue to mix for a further 8–10 minutes, until smooth and elastic. Now add the fruit and mix for 30 seconds until evenly spread throughout the dough. Remove the dough from the mixer and shape it into a round using your hands (the dough may be a bit hard to work with, but that's okay). Place it in a lightly oiled large bowl and cover with cling film or a clean tea towel.

...method continued on page 70

Leave the dough in a warm, draught-free spot for 45–60 minutes, until roughly doubled in size (although the exact time needed will depend on all sorts of factors, such as the freshness of your yeast and the temperature of your ingredients). Turn out the dough on to a lightly floured work surface and knock it back. Then, fold it into a rectangle and place it into the greased loaf tin. Leave the dough to prove, covered with a damp cloth, for about 30–45 minutes, until it has risen above the rim of the loaf tin.

In a small bowl combine the egg and milk for the egg wash and brush this over the top of the loaf. Place the loaf in the oven to bake for 20–25 minutes, until golden.

Remove from the oven and cool in the tin on a cooling rack for 5 minutes. Then, turn out the loaf and leave it on the rack until completely cooled.

To serve, cut the loaf into slices, toast lightly and spread with a healthy amount of butter. Top each with a slice of cheese, then place under a hot grill for a moment, just until the cheese starts to melt. Enjoy straight away.

I love the marriage of cheese, crackers and piccalilli. Weirdly I hated piccalilli when I was a child. My dad would sit and spoon it out of the jar at the table and the smell would make my stomach turn. But a few years later and here I am spooning it out of the jar with delight. It's great to store in the fridge and will keep for months.

The recipe for these crackers was created by Joeby Fowler, a chef at The Pony & Trap when I was Head Chef there in 2016. He rather brilliantly used the leftover sourdough from the restaurant to make these completely amazing crackers.

Homemade piccalilli & crackers
WITH CHEESE

SERVES 6

250g quality hard cheese

FOR THE PICCALILLI
1 cauliflower
2 large carrots
2 onions
30g sea salt, plus extra
   for the cucumber
1 cucumber
600ml cider vinegar
10g turmeric
10g mustard powder
100g caster sugar
50g runny honey
40g cornflour
1 teaspoon cumin seeds
1 teaspoon coriander seeds

FOR THE CRACKERS
250g plain flour
100g ground sourdough
   breadcrumbs
10g poppy seeds
10g black onion seeds
5g cumin seeds
50ml first-press rapeseed oil
4g salt

Cut the large florets off the cauliflower, then use a knife to cut those florets into smaller ones. The size of the vegetables for the piccalilli is down to you, but I would recommend cutting the onion and carrots into dice to match the cauliflower.

Combine the vegetables in a bowl and sprinkle with the salt. Give them a good shake and a squeeze, cover and leave overnight in a cool place. Drain off the excess liquid in the morning and give the vegetables a good squeeze again, but don't rinse them.

Halve the cucumber and scrape out the seeds with a spoon. Dice the flesh into 1cm pieces and sprinkle with salt, then add the pieces to the bowl with the vegetables.

Place the vinegar, turmeric, mustard powder, sugar and honey in a saucepan over a high heat and bring to the boil, then reduce the heat and simmer for 5 minutes to mellow.

In a bowl, add a little water to the cornflour to make a paste. Then, bit by bit add the hot vinegar liquid, whisking well as you do so to make sure there are no lumps. Pour the mixture back into the pan, and cook over a medium heat for about 2–3 minutes, until nicely thickened.

Lightly toast the cumin and coriander seeds in a dry frying pan over a medium heat until aromatic, then tip them into a spice grinder and pulse until crushed but not powdered (alternatively, crush them in a mortar with a pestle). Add the crushed seeds into the thickened vinegar mixture and then pour the mixture over the vegetables, folding through to finish. You can eat the piccalilli straight away, but it gets better with time (it will store for up to 6 months in the fridge).

...method continued on page 72

To make the crackers, preheat the oven to 195°C/175°C fan/Gas Mark 5.

Mix all the ingredients in a bowl with 200ml of water to create a dough. Place the dough in the fridge, cover with a damp cloth, and leave to rest and firm up for 30 minutes.

Roll out the dough between 2 sheets of baking paper until it is about 3mm thick. Transfer to a baking sheet, remove the top piece of baking paper and bake for 12–15 minutes, until crisp. Once cool, snap into good-sized pieces to create rustic crackers. Serve the piccalilli with cheese and crackers, for breakfast lunch or dinner – there's never a wrong time to serve cheese!

These Welsh cakes are very special to me, being one of my very first food memories. Doris is my great nan and she would make these Welsh cakes whenever the family visited her in Barry, Wales. My mum has carried on the tradition making Welsh cakes most weekends, always using Doris's griddle pan.

I like to serve them with a tangy Caerphilly, but they are just as good served on their own, fresh off the griddle with just a sprinkling of sugar and a steaming hot cup of tea.

Doris's Welsh cakes
& CAERPHILLY CHEESE

MAKES 24

120g cold unsalted butter, diced,
   plus extra for the griddle
225g plain flour
80g caster sugar
60g currants
1 egg, beaten
300g Caerphilly cheese, sliced,
   to serve

Put the butter and flour in a bowl and rub together until the mixture resembles breadcrumbs. Add the sugar and currants and combine. Make a well in the centre of the mixture and pour in the beaten egg. Using a spatula or wooden spoon, mix the egg into the dry ingredients, then work the mixture together with your hands to make a dough.

On a floured surface, roughly roll out the dough to 1cm thick. Using a 6cm pastry cutter (or any cutter you have to hand – just adjust the cooking time, if necessary), cut out as many Welsh cakes as you can, re-rolling the dough until you have used it all up.

Heat a griddle or frying pan until hot (as you would for cooking a pancake). Melt a little butter over the surface of the griddle or pan, just enough to coat the surface (you can use the butter wrapping, if you've finished the butter).

Cook the Welsh cakes in batches, giving them about 3 minutes on each side. (They are similar to pancakes – it can take a few to get them right, but persevere!)

They are best served warm, straight from the griddle or pan – enjoy with slices of Caerphilly cheese, but they are still delicious if you allow them to cool, then store them in an airtight container and have them cold the following day (or even a few days later).

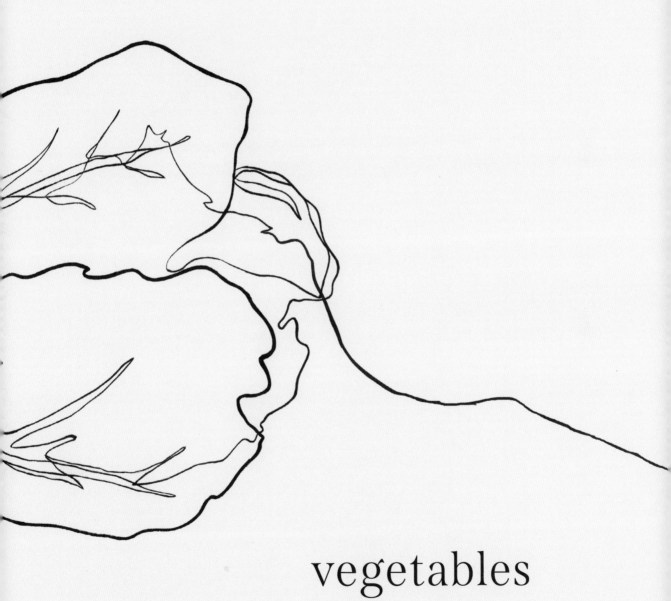

vegetables

This was the first dish on the menu at Root when we opened in 2017 and is the only dish that has never left. It's a dish full of wonderful flavour and texture and exemplifies what our restaurant is all about – showcasing vegetables to their best, giving them the respect they deserve and never wasting anything. It's not a quick dish to make but the fermented beetroot is well worth the effort and keeps really well, like all fermented food.

Beetroot
WITH BLACKBERRIES, HAZELNUTS & SEAWEED

SERVES 6

FOR THE FERMENT
1kg beetroot, peeled and grated, peel reserved
20g sea salt (or 2 per cent of the weight of the beetroot)

FOR THE BEETROOT MIXTURE
12 beetroot
1 punnet of blackberries (about 150g)
100g hazelnuts, roasted and crushed (see page 138)
pickle liquid (see page 258)
seaweed oil (see page 268), to serve
nasturtium leaves, to garnish
salt and freshly ground black pepper

For the ferment, place the grated beetroot in a large tray or bowl. Add the salt, massaging it into the beetroot, squeezing to release the juice. Continue until you have enough juice to cover the grated beetroot. (Expect this to take about 15 minutes, depending on how fresh your beetroot are.)

Transfer the mixture to a container (4-litre ice cream tubs are ideal) and cover with baking paper. Place another, similar container on top of the baking paper to press down on the grated beetroot ensuring that it is submerged in juice. Leave in a cool, dry place (a perfect temperature is 18–23°C) for 5 days to allow the beetroot to ferment. Transfer the mixture to an airtight container and refrigerate until you're ready to use it (it's fine until it's noticeably fizzy).

When you're ready to make the beetroot mixture, preheat the oven to 200°C/180°C fan/Gas Mark 6. Place 10 of the whole beetroots into a baking tray and roast them in the oven for about 3–4 hours, until they have shrivelled to about two-thirds their original size and are pulpy and rich.

Once the beetroot are ready, allow them to completely cool, then peel off the skins using your hands (they should come away easily). Roughly chop, transfer to a mixing bowl and put aside.

Roughly chop the blackberries and roasted hazelnuts, setting them aside in separate bowls.

Peel the remaining 2 beetroot and, using a mandolin, slice them into thin rounds. Spread these out on a baking tray and season well. Leave them to soften for 2 minutes, then place them into a bowl and cover them with pickle liquid.

Before serving, place 3 large tablespoons of the fermented beetroot into the bowl with the roasted beetroot (discard the skins). Stir through then transfer to a serving plate. Scatter the hazelnuts, blackberries and pickled beetroot over the top, then dress with some seaweed oil and a splash of the beetroot pickle liquid and finish with the nasturtium leaves.

I feel that aubergines are a bit undervalued in the domestic kitchen, perhaps because they need attention and love to bring out their best. This recipe certainly brings out the very best and though it may seem like quite a lot of work it's actually pretty easy and very, very delicious. The baba ganoush can be used alongside fish and meats or just served as a dip.

Grilled flatbreads
WITH BABA GANOUSH, KOHLRABI SLAW, PICKLED EWE'S CURD & DATES

SERVES 4

FOR THE BABA GANOUSH
5 aubergines
1 roasted garlic bulb (see page 267), flesh squeezed out
juice of 1 lemon
pinch of allspice, ground coriander or paprika
25ml sherry vinegar, plus extra to taste if necessary
10ml first-press rapeseed oil
salt and freshly ground black pepper

FOR THE SLAW
1 kohlrabi, peeled and cut into thin matchsticks
1 tablespoon rapeseed oil
1 tablespoon lemon juice
2 tablespoons chopped chives
salt

TO SERVE
1 aubergine, cut into 1cm pieces
4 tablespoons rapeseed oil
4 grilled flat breads (see page 256)
100g dates, chopped
100g feta-style cheese
1 pinch of sumac
10 mint leaves, chopped

For the baba ganoush, heat the grill to high. Using the end of a knife, prick the aubergines several times and place under the grill, cooking for roughly 20 minutes and turning every 5 minutes, until the skins are charred and the flesh is softened. Transfer the aubergines to a bowl, cover the top with cling film and leave to cool (about 5 minutes).

Once the aubergines have cooled, cut each in half lengthways and scoop out the flesh into a colander. Allow to drain, then roughly chop the flesh and put it into a mixing bowl.

Add the remaining baba ganoush ingredients and mix well using a whisk. Season to taste – be aware that aubergines can take a lot of salt and you may need a touch more vinegar to make the mixture nice and flavourful.

Prepare the aubergine to serve. Place the aubergine pieces in a colander and sprinkle with a good amount of salt. Leave for 5 minutes (or even overnight), then squeeze out any excess liquid.

Heat 2 tablespoons of the rapeseed oil in a frying pan over a high heat. When hot, add the aubergine pieces and fry for 3 minutes, tossing to turn, until the aubergine is softened and has taken on some colour. Taste for seasoning, then remove the pan from the heat and leave to the side until you're ready to serve.

Prepare the slaw. Add the kohlrabi to a mixing bowl. Sprinkle over some salt and leave it to sit for 5 minutes (or longer) to draw out some liquid. Drain the liquid from the bowl and add the rapeseed oil, lemon juice and chopped chives. Mix well, check the seasoning and set aside.

To assemble the dish, lay out the flat breads over a serving dish. Spoon over equal amounts of the baba ganoush and spread out, smoothing the surface. Top with a good amount of the slaw, then crumble over the cheese, chopped dates and finally the diced aubergine. Finish by drizzling over the remaining oil, and garnish with sprinklings of chopped mint and sumac.

I love artichokes; here the bitter chicory matched with the sweet pear, salty cheese and mildly acidic artichokes come together to create a deliciously balanced dish. Whilst fresh violet artichokes are quite time-consuming to prepare, the results will merit the effort. If time is an issue, then use the excellent cooked ones found in jars.

The poaching liquid will make more than you need, but you can use the remainder for the caramel cream and ginger crumble on page 232.

Braised chicory
WITH VIOLET ARTICHOKES, BLUE CHEESE & POACHED PEARS

SERVES 4

FOR THE POACHED PEARS
350ml white wine
250g caster sugar
1 teaspoon vanilla seeds
   (scraped from ½ vanilla pod)
1 star anise
1 bay leaf
zest and juice of 1 lemon
4 pears, peeled

FOR THE ARTICHOKE BARIGOULE
2 or 3 slices of lemon
a pinch of coarse sea salt
1 bunch of baby violet artichokes
4 tablespoons cooking oil
2 shallots, thinly sliced
1 carrot, peeled and sliced
1 garlic clove, sliced
1 thyme sprig
1 bay leaf
150ml chardonnay or other good-
   quality white wine vinegar, plus
   extra to prepare the artichokes
200ml white wine
100ml first-press rapeseed oil
juice of 1 lemon
salt

For the poached pears, place all the ingredients, apart from the pears, in a saucepan with 350ml water over a medium heat. Bring to the boil, then reduce the heat to a low simmer. Add the pears and cook for 5–15 minutes – the exact time will depend how ripe they are – until tender to the point of a knife, but giving a little resistance. Scoop out the pears into a suitable container and pour over the poaching liquid. Allow to cool, then cover with cling film and refrigerate until ready to serve.

Make the barigoule. First, fill a large bowl with some water (enough to hold all the artichokes) and add a couple of slices of lemon (to prevent them from discolouring) and the pinch of coarse sea salt. Set aside.

Peel off and discard the first 2–3 layers of outer leaves of each artichoke. Cut off the top half or two-thirds of each artichoke and trim the stalk. Cut away the remaining, tough leaves at the base and peel up the stalk to reveal a light part. Halve each artichoke and, using a teaspoon, scoop out and discard the hairy choke inside the heart. Place the prepared artichokes into the bowl of lemony salted water and set aside.

Heat the cooking oil in a saucepan over a medium heat. Add the shallots, carrot and garlic and allow to sweat for 2–3 minutes. Drain the artichokes and add them to the pan. Cook for about 3 minutes, until they take on some colour, then add the thyme, bay, vinegar and wine. Reduce the heat to a low simmer, add the rapeseed oil and lemon juice, then cover and simmer for 12–15 minutes, until the artichokes have softened. Remove from the heat and set aside.

While the artichokes are cooking, make the braised chicory. Cut the chicory in half lengthways and coat in the sugar. Heat the oil in a frying pan over a medium heat. Add the chicory halves cut-sides downwards and allow to caramelise slowly, cooking until they are a golden colour, and browning in places. Add the butter and allow to melt until foaming, then add the stock.

...ingredients & method continued on page 84

FOR THE BRAISED CHICORY
1 chicory
50g caster sugar
2 tablespoons cooking oil
50g unsalted butter
200ml vegetable stock

TO SERVE
1 conference pear, cored and sliced
1 chicory, leaves separated
150g Stilton or other blue cheese

Turn over the chicory halves and cook for a further 5 minutes, until cooked through and softened. Remove from the heat and leave to cool slightly before using.

To serve, quarter the poached pears and arrange 2 quarters on each plate. Spoon over the artichokes, including a little of the liquid, and the shallot mixture.

Cut each chicory half lengthways and add the quarters to the plate.

Place the slices of fresh pear in a bowl with the raw chicory leaves, dress with some of the artichoke liquid and add this equally to the 4 plates. Crumble over the blue cheese to finish.

This is a great dish full of wonderful flavours and textures, amazing on its own or paired with a cut of beef or grilled white fish. Be sure to get a good charring all over the artichoke for an extra flavour hit.

Jerusalem artichoke
WITH CELERIAC REMOULADE, ROASTED HAZELNUTS & SOAKED GOLDEN RAISINS

SERVES 4

FOR THE ARTICHOKE PURÉE
100ml rapeseed oil, plus extra
to finish the purée if needed
500g Jerusalem artichokes,
peeled and sliced
salt and freshly ground
black pepper

**FOR THE ARTICHOKE PICKLE AND
CRISPS**
500g Jerusalem artichokes
pickle liquid (see page 258)
rapeseed oil, for frying, plus
extra for rubbing
salt

FOR THE SOAKED RAISINS
200ml white wine
200g raisins

FOR THE REMOULADE
½ celeriac or 1 small celeriac,
peeled and cut into 2cm slices,
then into matchsticks
1 teaspoon wholegrain mustard
50ml rapeseed oil
50ml lemon juice
20ml sherry vinegar
2 tablespoons chopped chives

TO SERVE
100g hazelnuts, roasted and
crushed (see page 138)
chopped green herbs, such as
chervil (optional)

Make the purée. Heat the oil in a saucepan over a medium heat. When hot, add the artichoke slices, along with a good amount of salt, and cook, stirring well, for 5 minutes, until the artichokes colour and soften. Add 300ml of water and continue to cook for a further 5 minutes, until you are left with a little water and almost a purée. Place the contents of the pan in a blender and blitz well, adding a little more water if needed until smooth. Season to taste, and add a splash of rapeseed oil if you like – to make your purée nice and glossy. Set aside.

For the pickled artichokes, using a mandolin slice 4 artichokes into 2mm slices and put half of the slices into a bowl. Sprinkle with a generous amount of salt, then pour pickle liquid over the top to submerge.

For the crisps, heat a deep-fat fryer to 160°C. Add the remaining artichoke slices, stirring well for about 1 minute until they are evenly golden all over. Set aside to drain on kitchen paper, then when the excess oil has drained away and the crisps are dry, season well with salt.

For the soaked raisins, pour 200ml of water into a pan and place over a medium heat. Add the wine and raisins and bring to the boil. Reduce the heat and simmer gently for 5 minutes, until plump and nicely soaked, then remove from the heat, transfer to a bowl and cover with cling film. Leave to cool. When cooled, transfer to an airtight container and store in the fridge for up to 5 days (you'll have more than you need for this dish, but you can use them over anything from cauliflower couscous to various desserts).

For the remoulade, place the celeriac in a bowl and sprinkle with salt. Leave for 5 minutes, then squeeze the celeriac to remove the liquid. Drain the liquid from the bowl and add all the remaining remoulade ingredients, then mix well to combine. Set aside.

...method continued on page 86

Steam the remaining artichokes for about 25 minutes (the exact time will depend upon their size and variety), until soft to the point of a knife, but still holding their shape. (If you don't have a steamer, simmer the artichokes until soft.)

Heat the grill to high. Quarter or halve the artichokes and brush them with a good coating of oil. Transfer them to a grill pan and grill (in batches, if necessary) for about 5 minutes on each side, until charred and coloured all over. (The more colour, the better.)

To serve, spread equal amounts of the purée over 4 serving plates. Top each serving with a heaped spoonful of the remoulade, then grilled artichokes, pickled raisins and pickled artichokes. Finish with the artichoke crisps, hazelnuts and chopped herbs, if you wish.

The arrival of long summer days brings us all wonderful tomatoes to enjoy. And soaking up the juices from ripe tomatoes with freshly baked bread is one of life's great gastronomic pleasures and the inspiration for this dish. Make a batch of the delicious tomato and chilli jam to keep it in the fridge for the coming autumn and winter months.

Heritage tomatoes
WITH GRILLED FOCACCIA, AUBERGINE PURÉE & TOMATO JAM

SERVES 4

12 good-quality heritage tomatoes

FOR THE AUBERGINE PURÉE
5 aubergines
1 roasted garlic bulb (see page 267), flesh squeezed out
juice of 1 lemon
1 pinch of allspice, ground coriander or paprika
25ml sherry vinegar, plus extra to taste if necessary
10ml first-press rapeseed oil, plus extra for dressing the tomatoes
salt and freshly ground black pepper

FOR THE TOMATO CHILLI JAM
2 x 400g tins of chopped tomatoes
2 red chillies, deseeded and roughly sliced
2 banana shallots, sliced
2 garlic cloves
200ml white wine vinegar
400g caster sugar

TO SERVE
1 focaccia (see page 256)
8 basil leaves, torn
dried tomatoes (see page 270; optional)
2 tablespoons first-press rapeseed oil (optional)

For the aubergine purée, heat the grill to high. Using the end of a knife, prick the aubergines several times and place them under the grill, cooking for roughly 20 minutes and turning every 5 minutes, until the skins have blackened and the flesh is soft. Transfer the aubergines to a bowl, cover the top with cling film and leave to cool (about 5 minutes).

Once the aubergines have cooled, cut each in half lengthways and scoop out the flesh into a colander. Allow to drain, then add the flesh to a food processor. Add the remaining purée ingredients and blend to a thick purée. Season to taste – be aware that aubergines can take a lot of salt and you may need a touch more oil and some water to make a good purée. Set aside.

While the aubergines are grilling, make the tomato chilli jam. Tip the tomatoes into a colander and allow to drain slightly. Transfer to a blender and add all the remaining ingredients except the sugar. Blitz fully, then transfer to a saucepan. Place over a low–medium heat, add the sugar and cook for 15–20 minutes, until the mixture has reduced so that it is dark, thick and jam-like, taking care it doesn't catch during cooking. Blend again if you want your jam to be smoother. Set aside.

To prepare the heritage tomatoes, bring a pan of salted water to the boil and have a bowl of iced water on the side. Using a small knife, make a small 'x' cut on the bottom of each tomato and carefully remove the core. One by one, drop each tomato into the boiling water for 10 seconds to blanch, then remove with a slotted spoon and place straight into the iced water. Once you have blanched all the tomatoes, remove the skins and slice them however you wish. Transfer the slices to a bowl, dress with rapeseed oil and season with salt and pepper.

To serve, grill the focaccia to warm through, then cut it into generous pieces. Spoon the aubergine purée on to a serving plate, then arrange the chopped heritage tomatoes on top. Scatter over the torn basil leaves and a few dried tomatoes, if you have them. Dot the tomato chilli jam around the plate and maybe finish with a further splash of oil. Alternatively, toast the focaccia, spread the aubergine purée on top and add the tomatoes and basil – like a bruschetta. How you serve this dish is really up to you!

This brilliant recipe allows for a number of different flavoured risottos – simply alter the purée and the stock to suit. Mushroom, pumpkin and sweetcorn work well, but beetroot trumps them all – the colour and flavour of the beet is just so intense.

Beetroot risotto
FINISHED WITH GOAT'S CHEESE

SERVES 4

FOR THE BEETROOT PURÉE
750g peeled and sliced beetroot
500ml beetroot juice, plus extra
 (optional) to purée
50ml sherry vinegar, plus extra
 to taste, if necessary
100ml red wine
sea salt and freshly ground
 black pepper

FOR THE RISOTTO
800ml vegetable stock, plus
 extra if necessary
300ml beetroot juice
2 tablespoons cooking oil
2 shallots, peeled and diced
1 garlic clove, minced
1 roasted garlic bulb (see page
 267), flesh squeezed out
400g risotto rice
150ml red wine
50g cold unsalted butter
80g Parmesan, grated
lemon juice, to taste (optional)
100g soft goat's cheese, to serve
salt

For the beetroot purée, put all the ingredients into an extra-large saucepan. Add enough water to cover, along with a good pinch of salt, and place over a medium heat. Cook for about 30 minutes, until the beetroot are soft and most of the liquid has disappeared. Keep an eye on the pan as the beetroot can spit and it can get messy. Place the beetroot mixture into a blender and blitz until you have a smooth purée. If there is not enough liquid to achieve the right consistency, add a little water or extra beetroot juice. (You can make this in advance and store it in the fridge for up to 3 days, if you like. Freeze any leftovers – you may have too much for the risotto.)

For the risotto, pour the vegetable stock and beetroot juice into a saucepan and place over a gentle heat to keep warm.

In a separate pan, heat the oil in over a medium heat. When hot, add the shallots and both garlics and fry gently for about 5 minutes, or until the shallots are softened but not coloured. Add the rice and fry lightly for 1 minute, until slightly translucent. Add the red wine and keep stirring until absorbed.

Add your first ladleful of hot stock and a good pinch of salt. Reduce the heat to a simmer (this helps the rice cook evenly), and keep adding the stock one ladleful at a time, stirring continuously and allowing each ladleful to be absorbed before adding the next, until you have used all the stock. The whole process should take about 15 minutes, at which point you will have rice that still needs bit of cooking.

Add 6 tablespoons of beetroot purée to the risotto and taste. You will start to see your risotto come together now – if it needs a little more stock, add it but the purée might be enough to cook the rice until it's soft but with a slight bite.

Remove the pan from the heat and, using a wooden spoon or spatula, stir through the cold butter and the Parmesan. Taste for salt and pepper, and add a little lemon juice or an extra splash of sherry vinegar just to get the balance right if necessary. Serve as soon as possible with the goat's cheese crumbled over the top.

The British asparagus season is very short so be sure to make the most of it while you can. The almond sauce in this recipe is basically a slightly thicker version of Spain's classic ajo blanco. Try to find the very best-quality sherry vinegar – it will make the world of difference to the finished dish.

Asparagus
WITH FENNEL SALAD, SPICED ALMONDS & ALMOND SAUCE

SERVES 4

16 asparagus spears
chive oil (see page 268),
  or use rapeseed

FOR THE SPICED ALMONDS
1 tablespoon lightly whisked
  egg white
1 pinch of paprika
1 pinch of allspice
1 pinch of cayenne pepper
1 pinch of salt
1 teaspoon maple syrup
1 tablespoon rapeseed oil
200g whole blanched almonds

FOR THE ALMOND SAUCE
120g blanched almonds
50g slightly stale white bread
  (crusts removed)
1 garlic clove
1 pinch of salt
3 tablespoons sherry vinegar
100ml rapeseed oil

FOR THE FENNEL SALAD
1 fennel bulb
1 tablespoon chopped dill
1 tablespoon first-press
  rapeseed oil
a splash of chardonnay or other
  good-quality white wine vinegar
salt

Preheat the oven to 190°C/170°C fan/Gas Mark 5.

While the oven is heating, prepare the asparagus. Using a peeler, remove the fibrous part from the base of each spear to about 2–3cm up the stem. This will leave you with lovely, tender spears of asparagus. Set aside.

Make the spiced almonds. In a mixing bowl whisk together the egg white, spices, salt, maple syrup and rapeseed oil. Add the almonds and mix, making sure each nut is coated slightly. Spread out on a baking tray and bake for 15 minutes, giving the nuts a turn every 3 minutes to make sure you get a nice, even roast, until crispy and golden. Leave to cool. (You can make these in advance, if you like, and store them in an airtight container for up to 5 days.)

While the almonds are cooling, make the almond sauce. Place the almonds, bread, garlic and pinch of salt in a blender. Measure out 300ml of water and keep this and the rapeseed oil and sherry vinegar to hand. Start blending and slowly add the water, then the sherry vinegar and finish with the rapeseed oil. Stop blending and taste (the consistency should be somewhere between a purée and a soup), check for seasoning and transfer to a bowl until needed.

For the fennel salad, cut 1cm off the base of the fennel and cut the bulb in half lengthways. Use a mandolin to shave the fennel into thin slices. Place these in a mixing bowl. Add the dill, rapeseed oil, splash of vinegar and a nice pinch of salt and lightly toss. This is a lovely way to enjoy the fennel.

Bring a pan of salted water to the boil and drop in the prepared asparagus spears. Cook for 2 minutes, then remove them from the water, drain them and put them in a frying pan with 50ml of the chive (or rapeseed) oil. Place over a medium heat for another 2 minutes, until cooked.

Arrange the cooked asparagus on serving plates, dress with the almond sauce, scatter the nuts and fennel over and finish with a drizzle of the chive (or rapeseed) oil left in the pan.

This was a very early Root dish and is still a favourite, inspired by one-time Bristol restaurateurs Sam and Becky Leech. Sam and Becky now grow fruit and vegetables and supply our restaurant with amazing local produce. The raw button mushrooms may seem an unlikely partner, but they actually work wonderfully well with the fried eggs and the silky-smooth artichoke purée.

Mushroom duxelle
WITH ARTICHOKES, FRIED HEN'S EGGS & RAW BUTTON MUSHROOMS

SERVES 4

FOR THE MUSHROOM DUXELLE
500g flat field mushrooms
a little rapeseed oil
3 shallots, finely diced
2 garlic cloves, minced
1 thyme sprig, leaves picked
    and chopped
cep powder (optional)
truffle oil (optional)
salt and freshly ground
    black pepper

FOR THE ARTICHOKE PURÉE
100ml rapeseed oil, plus extra
    for frying the eggs
500g Jerusalem artichoke,
    peeled and thinly sliced

FOR THE ARTICHOKE CRISPS
5 Jerusalem artichokes, thinly
    sliced
cooking oil, for frying

TO SERVE
4 eggs
10 button mushrooms, finely sliced

For the duxelle, either hand chop, or pulse the mushrooms in a food processor to chop very finely, almost like a mushroom mince. Set aside.

Heat a little rapeseed oil in a saucepan over a medium heat. Add the shallots and garlic and allow to sweat for 5 minutes, until soft. Add the thyme, then the minced mushrooms. Sprinkle over the cep powder to taste (if using), then season with a nice amount of salt and pepper and add the truffle oil, if using. Cook on a low heat for 15–20 minutes, or until the mushrooms have released all their water and you are left with a nice mushroom pâté.

Make the purée. Heat the oil in a saucepan over a medium heat. When hot, add the artichoke slices, along with a good amount of salt, and cook, stirring well, for 5 minutes, until the artichokes colour and soften. Add 300ml of water and continue to cook for a further 5 minutes, until you are left with a little water and almost a purée. Place the contents of the pan in a blender and blitz well, adding a little more water if needed, until smooth. Season to taste, and add a splash of rapeseed oil if you like – to make your purée nice and glossy. Set aside.

Make the artichoke crisps. Heat a deep-fat fryer to 160°C. Add the artichoke slices, stirring well for about 1 minute, until they are evenly golden all over. Set aside to drain on kitchen paper, then, when the excess oil has drained away and the crisps are dry, season well with salt.

Just before serving, fry the eggs. Heat about 1cm depth of oil in a large frying pan over a low heat. Using cooking rings if you have them (otherwise the rustic look is fine), place the rings in the oil and crack in the eggs. Leave them to slowly cook for about 4–5 minutes, until the white is firm and the yolk still runny.

To serve, using cooking rings (if you have them), on each plate add a layer of duxelle to the bottom of each ring, smoothing out the surface with the back of a spoon. Next, add a layer of artichoke purée, followed by the fried egg. Top with a few artichoke crisps, then remove the rings and scatter over a few slices of button mushroom to finish. If you don't have cooking rings, simply plate up the layers as neatly as possible – it will still be delicious.

This is a perfect summer lunch, refreshing and hearty. Tomato water is basically blended and hung tomatoes, a technique which releases the most amazing flavour. It's greenhouse tomato flavour x 100! You will need to use either good ripe tomatoes or ones that have just sat around for a little too long.

Haricot beans in tomato water
WITH FRESH TOMATO & PICKLED FENNEL

SERVES 4

FOR THE HARICOT BEANS
200g dried haricot beans, soaked for 8 hours in water
1.5 litres vegetable stock
125ml white wine
2 bay leaves
3 thyme sprigs
salt

FOR THE TOMATO WATER
12 ripe tomatoes on the vine
2 basil sprigs
2 mint leaves
1 teaspoon peppercorns
1 teaspoon coriander seeds
1 teaspoon chardonnay or other good-quality white wine vinegar
1 garlic clove
1 thyme sprig, leaves picked
1 good pinch of salt

FOR THE TOMATOES AND FENNEL
1 fennel, thinly sliced
pickle liquid (see page 258)
4 tomatoes, roughly sliced
50ml salad dressing (see page 259)
parsley oil (see page 268), to serve
salt

First, cook the beans. Drain off the soaking water and place the beans in a saucepan. Add the remaining ingredients and a pinch of salt and place over a medium heat. (You can add more salt if you like, but we feel that the beans have a unique flavour that just needs enhancing.) Bring to the boil, then reduce the heat and simmer for 50–60 minutes, then taste to see if they're done: if they're still a little chalky in texture, cook on. When the beans are ready, remove the pan from the heat and leave the beans to cool in their cooking water. Season if necessary, then set aside in the liquid until needed. (The beans keep well in the fridge for 2 or 3 days and are great for breakfast, lunch or dinner.)

For the tomato water, roughly chop the tomatoes and some of the vine. Add the tomatoes and vine pieces to a blender along with the remaining ingredients and blitz well.

Line a sieve with a couple of overlapping J-cloths and suspend it over a bowl. Carefully pour in the tomato mixture. Place the sieve and bowl in the fridge and come back to it in an hour or so – you will have collected beautiful tomato water in the bowl. If you're not fussy about having a lovely, clear liquid, you can give the mixture in the sieve a bit of a squeeze to extract all of the juice – it will just make the collected water a little cloudy. Discard the contents of the sieve.

Place the sliced fennel in a bowl and pour over enough pickle liquid to cover. Set aside.

Place the sliced tomatoes in a mixing bowl and add the dressing, season with salt and mix well.

Using a slotted spoon transfer the beans (discarding the cooking water) to a serving bowl and add the tomatoes and fennel. Pour in the tomato water and drizzle over a little parsley oil to finish.

This fantastic curry sauce is reminiscent of a chicken korma, with its deliciously gentle spicy sweetness. It's versatile and is so good that I could almost drink it! The salt dough is also versatile and good not just for vegetables but for meat and fish too.

Salt baked celeriac & almond curry
WITH A CORIANDER & LIME DRESSING

SERVES 4

FOR THE BAKED CELERIAC
500g plain flour
165g table salt
2 egg whites
1 celeriac

FOR THE CORIANDER DRESSING
1 bunch of coriander
15 mint leaves
2 spring onions
juice of 2 limes
150ml rapeseed oil, plus extra
   for finishing the celeriac

FOR THE CURRY SAUCE
3 tablespoons cooking oil
2 shallots, sliced
1 roasted garlic bulb (see page
   267), flesh squeezed out
1 red chilli, deseeded and sliced
50g fresh ginger root, peeled
   and sliced
1 carrot, peeled and sliced
2 tablespoons mild curry powder
1 tablespoon turmeric powder
1 good pinch of salt
1 banana, sliced
2 apples, peeled, cored and sliced
100g blanched almonds
125ml white wine

First, make a salt dough for the baked celeriac. Mix the flour and salt together in a large bowl. Add the egg whites and 190ml of water. Stir with a spatula to form a firm dough, adding a little more water, if needed. Using your hands, knead the dough for a couple of minutes until smooth. Wrap the dough in cling film and rest in the fridge for 30 minutes or until needed.

Preheat the oven to 200°C/180°C fan/Gas Mark 6.

Turn out the dough on to a lightly floured work surface. Using a rolling pin, roll out the dough until large enough to fully encase the celeriac. The dough is very pliable, so feel free to use your hands to push it around the vegetable.

Place the wrapped celeriac on a baking tray and bake for 1½ hours, until the crust is rock solid and completely golden, then remove and leave to cool completely (about another 1 hour or 1½ hours), by which time the celeriac should be perfectly cooked.

Meanwhile, make the coriander dressing. Either place all the ingredients in a food processor and blitz until combined, or finely chop the herbs and spring onions, place them in a bowl and fold through the lime juice and rapeseed oil. Season well before transferring to an airtight container and refrigerating until needed.

Make the curry the sauce. Heat the oil in a heavy-based saucepan over a medium heat. Add the shallots, garlic, chilli, ginger and carrot. Cook on a medium heat for 2–3 minutes, stirring, then add the curry powder, turmeric and good pinch of salt. Sweat the vegetables for a further 5 minutes, until they start to colour (this is a good thing). Add the banana, apple and almonds, and cook for 2–3 minutes, until the apple has softened. Add the wine to deglaze the pan, stirring well to get any flavour off the bottom. Allow the wine to reduce by half (about 1 minute), then add 2 litres of water.

...method continued on page 100

Bring to the boil, then reduce the heat and allow to simmer for 20 minutes, until the contents of the pan are soft. Allow to cool slightly, then use a hand-held blender or food processor to blitz well. If the sauce is a little watery, once blended place it back on the heat and reduce to a sauce consistency.

Break away the salt-dough crust from the celeriac and remove the celeriac from the casing. Using a knife, remove the celeriac skin and, when cooled, tear apart the vegetable into natural chunks. Pour a little rapeseed oil in to a frying pan over a medium heat. When hot, add the celeriac pieces to the pan and fry for a good 5 minutes, until well coloured and seasoned.

Pour the sauce into the pan with the celeriac and serve the coriander dressing alongside. As a main course, serve with some rice.

I first made this dish for a guest chef night at Root. We wanted something simple and smart that we could make in advance and that couldn't go wrong on the night. It proved to be a great success and we have made them many more times since. A fair amount of work is involved in the prepping of the lattice but it's well worth the effort and they are a joy to eat.

Onion, leek, celeriac & Jerusalem artichoke lattice
WITH VEGETABLE GRAVY

SERVES 10–12 (MAKES 2)

1kg Jerusalem artichokes
3 tablespoons cooking oil
1 tablespoon sherry vinegar, plus
    extra to taste if needed
6 onions, sliced
4 leeks, sliced
1 celeriac, peeled and cut into
    2–3cm dice
4 tablespoons first-press
    rapeseed oil
3 thyme sprigs, leaves picked
2 garlic cloves, crushed
75g dried breadcrumbs
    (ideally panko)
truffle oil, to taste (optional)
sherry vinegar (optional)
2 x 500g blocks of puff pastry
1 x 320g sheet ready-rolled puff
    pastry (optional), for the lattice
2 eggs, beaten, for the egg wash
salt and freshly ground black
    pepper

FOR THE GRAVY
3 tablespoons cooking oil
2 onions, sliced
1 teaspoon ground coriander,
    plus optional extra to flavour
    the filling
1 teaspoon paprika, plus optional
    extra to flavour the filling
1 teaspoon allspice, plus optional
    extra to flavour the filling

Make the purée. Peel and slice 500g of the artichokes. Heat 1 tablespoon of the cooking oil in a large saucepan over a high heat. When hot, add the sliced artichokes and season with a good amount of salt. Cook, stirring frequently to prevent catching, for about 8–10 minutes, until you've got good colour on the artichokes (more colour, better flavour).

Cover the artichokes with water and bring to the boil. Cook over a medium heat for about 5 minutes, until most of the liquid has evaporated and the artichokes are tender. Remove from the heat, transfer to a food processor and blitz to a thick purée. Add the sherry vinegar and check the seasoning. (The purée will help to keep your filling nice and moist.)

In a large saucepan heat the remaining 2 tablespoons of cooking oil over a medium heat. Add the sliced onions and reduce the heat to medium–low. Cook very slowly, stirring occasionally, for about 25–30 minutes, until the onions are a nice golden brown colour. Remove from the heat and transfer to a large bowl to cool.

While the onions are cooking and cooling, make the gravy. Heat the cooking oil a large saucepan over a medium–high heat. When hot, add the sliced onions, season with salt, and cook for about 6–8 minutes, until the onions have taken on a good amount of colour. Add the spices and onion powder, then add the mushrooms and cook for a further 6 minutes or so, until the mushrooms are well-coloured, too. Add the Marmite, Worcestershire sauce and vinegar and cook for 2–3 minutes, until reduced by two-thirds. Add the porter or stout and bring to the boil. Boil for about 2–3 minutes, until reduced again by one-third, then add the vegetable stock. Return the gravy to the boil and allow to bubble away until reduced again by a half, then remove from the heat. Using a hand-held stick blender, blitz the gravy until smooth and glossy. Add a little more vegetable stock or water to adjust the consistency, if necessary. Set aside until you're ready to serve.

Bring a large saucepan of salted water to the boil. Have a small bowl of iced water ready at the side. Add the sliced leeks to the boiling water and blanch for 30 seconds, then using a sieve to scoop them out, transfer them straight

... ingredients & method continued on page 102

1 teaspoon onion powder
250g button mushrooms, sliced
2 tablespoons Marmite
1 tablespoon Worcestershire
  sauce
1 tablespoon red wine vinegar
500ml porter or stout
1 litre vegetable stock

into the iced water (leave the water on the boil). Drain very well, giving the leeks an extra squeeze to remove any excess moisture (the filling will won't hold if the leeks are too wet). Add the leeks to the cooked onion in the bowl.

Preheat the oven to 220°C/200°C fan/Gas Mark 7.

Place the celeriac pieces in the pan with the boiling water and cook for 2 minutes, then scoop them out with a sieve or slotted spoon and scatter them over a baking tray. Add the remaining, whole artichokes to the boiling water and cook for 4 minutes, then drain (you can discard the water this time). Cut the artichokes into halves, or quarters if large, and add them to the baking tray with the celeriac.

Sprinkle over the rapeseed oil, season with salt and pepper, then add the thyme and crushed garlic. Bake for 12 minutes, until both vegetables are well coloured and soft. Drain off any excess liquid from the tray and add the vegetables to the large bowl with the onions and leeks.

Add the breadcrumbs to the bowl, along with enough of the artichoke purée to bind the mixture together well (you may not need all the purée – use any remaining to stir through or serve with other dishes, such as a risotto). Taste for seasoning – you can add some extras such as truffle oil, sherry vinegar or spices at this point, if you wish.

On a large counter surface lay out 3 layers of cling film. Halve the filling and place it on the cling film, then roll it nice and tightly into a cylinder about 30cm long, making sure there is as little air as possible in the roll. Repeat with the other half of the filling and place both rolls in the freezer to firm up for at least 30 minutes, but longer if you wish. (This will make it easier to slice.)

Preheat the oven to 210°C/190°C fan/Gas Mark 6–7. Roll out one block of the puff pastry on a lightly floured worktop until it is a rectangle about 3mm thick and about 40cm long. Remove the rolls from the freezer and unwrap them from the cling film. Place one roll in the sheet of pastry and fold the pastry over to encase. Repeat for the other block of pastry and the second roll. Trim at the long edges and at the ends, then turn the rolls seam-sides downwards on a baking tray lined with baking paper and seal the edges with a little egg wash. Refrigerate for 10–15 minutes before cooking.

If you want to lattice the rolls, unroll the ready-rolled sheet of puff pastry and using a lattice cutter, make the pastry lattice to place on top of each roll.

Egg wash the chilled rolls, making sure that there are no breakages in the pastry. Bake for 25–30 minutes, until the pastry is golden and crisp.

While the rolls are baking, warm the gravy. Slice and serve simply with the gravy and with greens on the side.

This is a winter warmer, perfect for a dark and rainy day. We came up with this dish whilst trying to recreate a similar depth of flavour and nourishing joy that a beef stew gives – and I think we succeeded. The dumplings are rich and sweet, the roasted celeriac broth really gives you those lovely meaty notes and the chive oil helps bring the whole dish to life.

Celeriac & cider broth
WITH THYME DUMPLINGS, PAN-TOASTED CELERIAC & PICKLED CELERY

SERVES 4

FOR THE CELERIAC BROTH
2 tablespoons cooking oil,
  plus 1 tablespoon for the
  pan-roasted celeriac
1 shallot, sliced
1 garlic clove, chopped
1 roasted garlic bulb (see page
  267), flesh squeezed out
1 bay leaf
4 thyme sprigs
1 celeriac, peeled and cut
  into about 2cm dice
1 good pinch of salt, plus
  extra to season
500ml cider
1 teaspoon chardonnay or other
  good-quality white wine vinegar
freshly ground black pepper

FOR THE THYME DUMPLINGS
50g vegetable suet
110g self-raising flour
generous ½ teaspoon salt
½ teaspoon ground black pepper
1 tablespoon chopped
  thyme leaves
½ teaspoon mustard powder

FOR THE PICKLED CELERY
3 celery sticks, diced
pickle liquid (see page 258)

TO SERVE
2 tablespoons chopped chives
chive oil (see page 268)

For the broth, heat the cooking oil in a large saucepan over a medium heat. Add the shallot, both garlics, the herbs and three-quarters of the diced celeriac to the pan with a nice pinch of salt, adding more oil if the pan looks dry. Increase the heat to high and, stirring every couple of minutes, cook for about 15 minutes, making sure you get a nice even colour on the celeriac, until you have a lovely-smelling pan and the celeriac is soft and caramelised.

Deglaze the pan with the cider and cook for a further 2 minutes, then add 3 litres of water. Reduce the heat and cook for 30 minutes, until the liquid has reduced to just over 1 litre.

While the celeriac broth is simmering, make the dumplings. Put all the ingredients into a mixing bowl and rub the mixture through your fingers until the suet is evenly distributed. Slowly add 90ml of water, mixing well until you are left with a rollable dough. Roll the dough into 15g balls (each about the size of a walnut – about 14 balls) and set aside.

When the broth is ready, pass the mixture through a sieve or chinois into a clean pan, really pushing the vegetables with the back of a ladle to get the most flavour out of them. Stir in the vinegar and season to taste.

Add the dumplings to the hot broth and cover the pan. Cook the dumplings in the broth for about 15 minutes, turning them halfway through the cooking time, until they have tripled in size and are light and fluffy, but retaining a little firmness.

While the dumplings are cooking, heat the 1 tablespoon of cooking oil in a frying pan and add the remaining diced celeriac. Fry (pan-roasting) for 2 minutes, until the celeriac is nicely coloured, then remove from the pan and set aside.

For the pickled celery, simply place the celery into a small bowl and pour over the pickling liquid. Keep in the liquid until needed.

Ladle the broth and dumplings equally into serving bowls and add the diced celeriac. Drain the celery and add that, too. Finish with chopped chives and a drizzle of chive oil.

Sharpham Park is a 300-acre historic park near Glastonbury in Somerset, dating back to the Bronze Age, whose wonderful produce is now widely available in supermarkets. I toast our Sharpham Park spelt before using which gives it an amazing nutty flavour. Pearl barley is a great alternative for the spelt, and if you are lucky enough to get your hands on some wild mushrooms, even better!

Chilli & ginger Sharpham Park spelt
WITH CHESTNUT MUSHROOMS

SERVES 4

FOR THE SPELT
250g Sharpham Park spelt
3 tablespoons cooking oil
1 red chilli, deseeded and diced
80g fresh ginger root, peeled
    and diced
2 shallots, diced
1 garlic clove, chopped
1 tablespoon white miso
    paste (optional)
125ml white wine
1 litre hot vegetable stock
2 handfuls of frozen peas
1 teaspoon dark soy sauce
1 teaspoon sherry vinegar
1 teaspoon lemon juice
3 tablespoons chopped coriander

FOR THE MUSHROOMS
2 tablespoons cooking oil
200g chestnut mushrooms, diced
1 knob of unsalted butter (optional)
salt and freshly ground
    black pepper

TO SERVE
150g mushrooms, thinly sliced

Preheat the oven to 190°C/170°C fan/Gas Mark 5. Spread out the spelt on a baking tray and roast in the oven for 14 minutes, stirring half way through the cooking time, until toasted. Remove from the oven and leave to cool.

Heat the oil in a heavy-based saucepan over a medium heat. Add the chilli, ginger, shallots and garlic. Allow to sweat for 5 minutes, stirring well, until everything is tender. Then, add the toasted spelt and the miso (if using) and continue stirring. Add the wine to deglaze the pan and cook until all the wine has been absorbed (about 1 minute). Just as with a risotto, add the stock one ladleful at a time, allowing each ladleful to absorb before adding the next. After 15–20 minutes, the spelt will swell, having taken most of the stock if not all of it, and you will be left with a pan of lovely, cooked grains. Set aside. (If you aren't intending to finish the dish straight away, spread the spelt out on a baking tray to cool.)

To make the mushrooms, heat the oil in a frying pan over a high heat. Add the chestnut mushrooms and season well (mushrooms do need it). Fry for about 1 minute (the exact time will depend on the size of the mushrooms), until soft and golden, then add the knob of butter, if you wish, to finish.

Add the peas, soy, sherry vinegar, lemon juice and coriander to the spelt and stir to combine.

To serve, spoon equal amounts of the spelt mixture on to 4 plates, add the chestnut mushrooms and top with the thinly sliced raw mushrooms to finish.

This is a great big dish of chunky tasty vegetables. The salt baking method is a great way to treat beets, intensifying both their flavour and their colour, and it's a technique that can be used for a whole variety of your favourite root vegetables.

Salt-baked beetroot
WITH TURNIPS, SMOKED YOGHURT & SAVOURY WALNUT GRANOLA

SERVES 4

FOR THE SAVOURY GRANOLA
150g old-fashioned oats
50g walnut halves
50g sunflower seeds
2 tablespoons sesame seeds
2 tablespoons cumin seeds
2 tablespoons mustard seeds
1 pinch of cayenne pepper
1 pinch of salt
3 tablespoons first-press
  rapeseed oil
2 tablespoons agave syrup
2 tablespoons maple syrup

FOR THE BAKED VEGETABLES
500g plain flour
165g table salt
2 egg whites
4 beetroot, tops removed
  and reserved
4 turnips, tops removed
  and reserved

TO SERVE
500g smoked yoghurt
  (see page 263)
2 tablespoons first-press
  rapeseed oil
4 pickled walnuts, from a jar
2 tablespoons salad dressing
  (see page 259)

First, make the granola. Preheat the oven to 180°C/160°C fan/Gas Mark 4. Place all the dry granola ingredients in a mixing bowl. In another bowl, whisk together the oil, and the agave and maple syrups. Pour the wet mixture over the oat mixture and mix well until everything is coated evenly. Spread the mixture on a tray lined with baking paper and bake for 10 minutes. Remove from the oven, give everything a stir and return to the oven to bake for another 10 minutes, or until golden and crisp. Remove from the oven and allow to cool. (You can store the granola in an airtight container in a cool, dry place for up to 5 days, if you like.)

Make the salt dough for the baked vegetables. Mix the flour and salt together in a large bowl. Add the egg whites and 190ml of water. Stir with a spatula to form a firm dough, adding a little more water, if needed. Using your hands, knead the dough for a couple of minutes until smooth. Wrap the dough in cling film and refrigerate for 30 minutes, or until needed.

Preheat the oven to 200°C/180°C fan/Gas Mark 6.

Turn out the dough on to a lightly floured work surface. Using a rolling pin, roll out the dough until large enough to create a piece that will wrap fully around the 4 beetroots in one parcel and around the 4 turnips in another parcel. The dough is very pliable, so feel free to use your hands to push it around the vegetables. Place both parcels on a lined baking tray and bake for 30–40 minutes for the turnips and 45–60 minutes for the beetroots, depending on the size, until tender, then remove from the oven and leave to cool. (To check the vegetables during the process, stick a knife in through the dough casing to check firmness – the vegetables should yield to the knife when they are ready.)

When cooled, break open the salt crusts and peel away the skins of both the beetroot and turnips. Roughly chop up the cooked vegetables, and set aside in separate bowls.

To serve, spread some smoked yoghurt over each plate. Sprinkle the turnip and beetroot with a little rapeseed oil, then spoon equal amounts of each on to the bed of yoghurt. Cut the pickled walnuts into 4 and add the slices to each plate. Sprinkle over the walnut granola. Toss the turnip and beetroot tops in the dressing and use these to finish each plate.

These gnudi dumplings are excellent when you fancy a tasty, easy dinner. You will need to plan ahead though as the dumplings need to sit overnight to settle. But come the day, or the evening, they will take just a matter of minutes to whip up and put on the table. I like to use an ewe's curd rather than the traditional ricotta as it gives a slightly lighter result, but you can use either and it will still be delicious.

You will need to start this recipe a day before you plan to eat it!

Ewe's curd dumplings
WITH ROMESCO SAUCE & KOHLRABI

SERVES 4

FOR THE EWE'S CURD DUMPLINGS
500g ewe's curd or ricotta
100g Parmesan, grated
zest of ½ and juice of
   1 unwaxed lemon
12g salt, plus extra to season
5g cracked black pepper, plus
   extra to season
500g semolina

FOR THE ROMESCO SAUCE
30g roasted almonds (see
   page 144)
30g roasted hazelnuts (see
   page 138)
200g tinned plum tomatoes,
   drained
125g roasted red peppers
   from a jar
¼ garlic clove
½ roasted garlic bulb (see page
   267), flesh squeezed out
½ teaspoon paprika
¼ teaspoon cayenne pepper
1 tablespoon sherry vinegar
1 tablespoon first-press
   rapeseed oil

FOR THE KOHLRABI
1 large kohlrabi, tough outer layer
   removed, flesh thinly sliced
1 teaspoon chopped chives
2 tablespoons rapeseed oil

Make the ewe's curd dumplings. Put the curd or ricotta, and the Parmesan, lemon zest and juice in a bowl. Add the salt and pepper and mix well, seasoning with a little more salt and pepper if you like. Refrigerate for at least 1 hour (the mixture is easier to turn into balls when it's cold).

Place all but a handful of the semolina evenly into a baking tray to create a good layer.

Remove the ricotta mixture from the fridge and, piece by piece, roll it between your hands to create 24 balls (each roughly the size of a walnut). Place the balls into the tray of semolina, giving them all a good shake to coat well. Refrigerate for 12–16 hours, shaking a couple of times during chilling, and add a little of the extra semolina if needed to stop the balls sticking.

To make the romesco, place the nuts in a food processor and blitz to a breadcrumb texture (you don't want to over-blitz so that you have nut butter, but nor do you want them too chunky). Transfer to a large mixing bowl, then put the drained tomatoes and peppers into the food processor with the rest of the ingredients and blend well. Add this to the bowl with the nuts and whisk to combine. Season with salt and pepper. Transfer to a saucepan and set aside.

Place the kohlrabi into a mixing bowl and sprinkle with salt. Mix well and leave for 5 minutes, to soften the kohlrabi and remove some of the liquid. Drain away the liquid then sprinkle in the chives and oil, and stir to combine.

When you're ready to serve, gently heat the romesco in a saucepan over a low heat, stirring it once in a while.

Prepare a steamer, or bring a pan of water to the boil, and add the dumplings. Steam or boil for 3 minutes, until cooked through. (You can also do this in a deep-fat fryer, if you wish.)

To serve, add an equal amount of romesco to each plate. Top with equal amounts of the dumplings and finish with the dressed kohlrabi.

This dish is a joyous celebration of the arrival of spring. The winter months are a fast passing memory and green shoots are showing all around. Jersey Royals are such beautiful potatoes with a unique flavour. If you can't be bothered to make the pea purée then the Jerseys will still be great simply served with good butter, fresh peas and some locally growing wild garlic – a true spring feast.

Jersey Royal potatoes
WITH PEAS, WILD GARLIC & CRÈME FRAÎCHE

SERVES 4

1kg Jersey Royal potatoes
2 bay leaves
2 thyme sprigs
2 mint sprigs
2 garlic cloves, crushed
10g salt
2 tablespoons cooking oil
2 shallots, diced
200g fresh peas
25g unsalted butter
2 tablespoons chopped chives
2 tablespoons chopped
   flat-leaf parsley
2 handfuls of wild garlic
4 tablespoons crème fraîche

FOR THE PEA PURÉE
50ml rapeseed oil
1 shallot, sliced
1 garlic clove, sliced
600ml vegetable stock
375g frozen peas
salt and freshly ground
   black pepper

Place the potatoes in a large saucepan with enough cold water just to cover them. Add the bay, thyme and mint sprigs, and the crushed garlic and salt. (Feel free to use other aromatics, if you wish – just any that you have available. For example, parsley, rosemary and oregano would all work, too.) Place the pan over a medium heat and bring to a low simmer. Cook the potatoes gently for 20–25 minutes, until just tender to the point of a knife. (They will continue to cook a little once you've drained them, so you don't want them too soft.) Drain and leave to cool in the colander.

To make the pea purée, heat the rapeseed oil in a large saucepan over a high heat. When hot, add the shallot and garlic, season with a touch of salt and fry for 2–3 minutes, until softened. Add the vegetable stock and bring to the boil. Add the peas and season again with salt and this time pepper, too. Take the pan off the heat and drain the peas, reserving the stock.

Set aside 100ml of the reserved stock in a jug. Put the peas in a food processor, add a little of the remaining stock liquid and blend. Keep adding stock through the feed tube little by little until you have a lovely, smooth pea purée. If you want an extra-smooth consistency, pass the purée through a sieve, but it's not essential. Check the seasoning and cool the purée as quickly as possible – transferring it to a bowl and setting it inside a larger bowl filled with ice and placing in the fridge is a good way to do this. Chill until needed. (It also keeps well for 2–3 days in the fridge and freezes well.)

Heat the cooking oil in a large frying pan over a medium heat. When hot, add the shallots and fry for 30 seconds, then add the cooled potatoes and season with salt and pepper. Add the fresh peas and the reserved 100ml of stock, and bring to the boil. Reduce to a simmer, then add the butter, herbs and wild garlic (reserve a few wild garlic flowers for garnish). Stir through the pea purée, adding enough to coat the potatoes and to create a nice saucy pan of green goodness (you can use any remaining purée as a soup or to serve with fish). Check the seasoning one last time and transfer to a serving bowl. Garnish with wild garlic flowers and serve with the crème fraîche on top.

This is a favourite dish at Root that shows off just how wonderful and tasty a roasted cauliflower can be. I like to make the cauliflower the centre piece of the table allowing everyone to dig in and marvel at the fantastic caramelised flavours.

Cauliflower steak, shaved salad & purée
WITH A CASHEW NUT CREAM

SERVES 4

2 cauliflowers
3 tablespoons cooking oil
1 good pinch of salt, plus
    extra to season
2 tablespoons first-press
    rapeseed oil
zest and juice of ½ unwaxed lemon
freshly ground black pepper

FOR THE CASHEW CREAM
250g cashews
1 pinch of salt
1 tablespoon rapeseed oil

Preheat the oven to 180°C/160°C fan/Gas Mark 4.

Start with the cashew cream. Spread out the cashew nuts in a baking tray and bake for 12–15 minutes, tossing them halfway through, until evenly coloured all over. Remove from the oven and leave to cool.

Once cool, place three-quarters of the nuts in a food processor along with the pinch of salt. Crush the remaining nuts using the base of a saucepan and set aside for the salad.

Blitz the nuts in the processor on high, adding 200ml of water through the feed tube, until the mixture is smooth and creamy. Keep processing, adding the rapeseed oil with the motor running. Check the seasoning for salt, then transfer to an airtight container and refrigerate until needed.

To prepare the cauliflower, remove the leaves from the cauliflowers but keep the stems intact. From the central parts of each cauliflower, cut 2 cross-sections 1.5–2cm thick to create 4 'cauliflower steaks'. Set aside. Using a mandolin or grater, shave the remaining florets into thin pieces. Set aside a small bowlful of the shavings for the salad.

Heat 2 tablespoons of the cooking oil in a heavy-based saucepan over a medium heat. Add all the cauliflower except the reserved cauliflower steaks and the bowlful of shavings. Add the salt and allow the cauliflower to sweat for 5–8 minutes, until you have a good amount of caramelisation in the pan. Add enough water to cover, then bring to the boil and cook for about 5 minutes, until the cauliflower is soft and most of the liquid has gone. Using a slotted spoon, and reserving the remaining cooking liquid in the pan, transfer the mixture to the food processor and blitz until smooth and creamy (add some of the remaining cooking liquid to achieve the right consistency, if necessary). Season to taste.

...method continued on page 118

Increase the oven to 200°C/180°C fan/Gas Mark 6.

Heat the remaining cooking oil in a frying pan over a medium heat. Season the cauliflower steaks with salt and pepper just as you would a meat steak. Add the slices to the hot oil in the pan and cook for 4 minutes altogether, turning the slices and basting with the oil regularly during cooking, until lightly golden on both sides. Transfer the slices to a baking tray and further cook in the oven for 6–8 minutes, until the steaks are a deeper golden colour and are tender. Set aside to keep warm while you make the salad.

Mix the reserved cauliflower shavings with the rapeseed oil, lemon zest and juice, and crushed, roasted cashews. Season with salt. To serve, place a generous spoonful of the warm cauliflower purée on to each plate. Top with the shaved salad, drizzle over the cashew cream and finish with the cauliflower steaks.

Gnocchi are great fun to make! At the restaurant we make them twice a week in very large quantities and I still love the process. This recipe gives enough for 10–12 good portions and freezes very well, so plan ahead and get creative. Once made you will have some very tasty, easy meals to hand. Try them with the spiced butter on page 38 and some greens, or the ox cheek ragu on page 212 with some fresh tomatoes.

Potato gnocchi

SERVES 10–12

8 large Maris piper potatoes
300g type 00 flour, plus
    extra for dusting
28g salt, plus extra for sprinkling
150g Parmesan, grated
2 eggs beaten with 2 egg yolks
2 tablespoons cooking oil

Preheat the oven to 200°C/180°C fan/Gas Mark 6.

Prick the potatoes all over with a fork, then place them on a baking tray. Sprinkle them with salt, then bake for 90 minutes, until the skins are crisp and the flesh is until tender.

Combine the flour, salt and Parmesan in a large mixing bowl.

Cool the cook potatoes for about 20 minutes, until they are cool enough to handle. Remove and discard the skins, then, one by one, put the potato flesh through a ricer into a bowl. (If you don't have a potato ricer, grate the potatoes against the fine side of a box grater.)

Weigh out 550g of the mashed potato. (You can use any leftover for fishcakes or just mashed potato.)

Transfer the weighed-out smooth potato to the bowl with the flour mixture. Add the beaten eggs and yolks and, using your hands, bring the mixture together (it will be wet to start with, but it will come together well). Get all you can off your hands and then give them a good wash.

Turn out the dough on to a flour-dusted work surface (you'll need quite a large working area, so clear the decks). Break off chunks of the dough and, using your hands, roll into a long rope about the diameter of an index finger. Repeat for the remaining dough. Cut each rope along its length to make roughly 2cm gnocchi. Arrange these in a single layer on a floured tray (you may need more than one). If you have 2 gnocchi paddles, roll the dough between the paddles to leave little dents. (Just leave the gnocchi as little pillows if you don't have any paddles.)

Fill a large saucepan with slightly salted water and bring to the boil over a high heat. Have a big bowl of iced water ready for cooling the gnocchi after cooking.

...method continued on page 120

Drop about 20 gnocchi at a time into the boiling water and cook for roughly 4–5 minutes, until the gnocchi float and sit on the surface of the water (the sign that they are cooked). Scoop out the cooked gnocchi with a sieve and tip them straight into the iced water to cool. Repeat until all the gnocchi are cooked and cooled.

(At this point, you can drain the cooled gnocchi in a colander and transfer them to airtight containers to store in the fridge or freezer.)

To cook, heat 2 tablespoons of cooking oil in a frying pan over a medium heat. Add the gnocchi, and cook for about 4–5 minutes, turning frequently to colour on both sides. Serve with your choice of sauce or garnish.

Cabbage is a tainted vegetable that has got itself a bad rep! The hispi cabbage is probably the sweetest of the cabbages and I'd recommend using it if you find yourself trying to sway any cabbage pessimists. The key to this recipe is the perfect balance between the charred flavour of the cabbage, the richness of the butter sauce and the acidity of the shallots, bringing them all together to create one delicious and harmonious dish. Seaweed and seaweed flakes are now widely available in most supermarkets and health stores and can be a great addition to your kitchen repertoire.

You can make this recipe without the seaweed vinegar, replacing it with a chardonnay or champagne vinegar, if you prefer. The recipe will make more than you need for this dish, as it is great to have around and lasts well.

Charred hispi cabbage
WITH SEAWEED BUTTER SAUCE, PICKLED SHALLOTS & FRESH RADISH

SERVES 4

2 shallots, thinly sliced
1 pinch of salt, plus extra to season pickle liquid (see page 258)
2 hispi cabbages, tough outer leaves discarded, halved (or quartered if large)
2 tablespoons salad dressing (see page 259) or first-press rapeseed oil
1 bunch of radishes, leaves discarded, thinly sliced, to serve

FOR THE SEAWEED VINEGAR
5 nori sheets
1 tablespoon seaweed flakes
650ml white wine vinegar
100g caster sugar

FOR THE BUTTER SAUCE
80ml seaweed vinegar (or white wine vinegar)
120ml white wine
25ml double cream
125g unsalted butter, diced and chilled
1 pinch of seaweed flakes
1 tablespoon lemon juice
freshly ground black pepper

First, make the vinegar. Place all the vinegar ingredients into a large saucepan with 350ml of water and bring to the boil. Whisk well, remove from the heat and cover with cling film. Leave to infuse for at least 1 hour or up to 12 hours. Strain the infused liquid through a fine sieve or a J-cloth to extract the seaweed vinegar. Transfer to a sterilised jar and store in the fridge for up to 6 weeks, using as needed.

Place the shallot slices in a bowl with the pinch of salt, then pour over the pickling liquid. Set aside.

Bring a pan of salted water to the boil and have a bowl of iced water ready. Boil the cabbage pieces, making sure they are fully submerged in the water, for 3–4 minutes, until tender. Transfer to the iced water to chill, then drain, pat dry and store until needed. (They keep well in the fridge for 2–3 days if you want to make ahead.)

To make the butter sauce, place the vinegar and wine in a saucepan over a medium heat. Allow to simmer for 3 minutes, until reduced by two-thirds. Add the cream, cook for 1 minute, then whisk in the diced butter. Once smooth and combined, add the seaweed flakes and lemon juice and season with salt and pepper. Don't let the sauce get too hot or too cold, as it will split. Set aside and keep warm while you finish the cabbage.

Coat the hispi cabbage pieces with a little dressing or rapeseed oil and sprinkle with salt and pepper to season. Heat a griddle, chargrill or frying pan to hot. Add the cabbage pieces and cook on each side for about 5 minutes, until really charred with the outsides of the cabbage almost blackened (this is what brings the flavour to the dish).

Arrange the cabbage pieces on a serving dish and pour over the sauce. Sprinkle with the pickled shallots and radish slices.

A marrow wasn't on my radar until I launched Root and began to experiment with finding a recipe that could bring out the best in this most underused of vegetables. This is the recipe I came up with using all the great flavours to be found in a pesto. A great review we had said 'I've never seen someone make a marrow so sexy'! Perfect as a simple lunch or as a great accompaniment to a main meal.

When using the preserved lemons make sure to slice them nice and thinly into small pieces as they have an extremely strong flavour. If used too liberally, preserved lemon can ruin a dish.

Grilled marrow
WITH PRESERVED LEMON, PARMESAN, PINE NUTS & BASIL

SERVES 4

50g pine nuts
200ml cooking oil
3 garlic cloves, sliced wafer thin
1 marrow, cut into 3cm slices
3 teaspoons salad dressing
    (see page 259) or first-press
    rapeseed oil
100g Parmesan, grated
10 basil leaves, torn
¼–½ preserved lemon (see page
    264), very thinly sliced
salt and freshly ground
    black pepper

Preheat the oven to 180°C/160°C fan/Gas Mark 4. Spread the pine nuts over a baking tray and roast in the oven for 15–18 minutes, or until golden, giving them a shake halfway through cooking, until they are golden all over. Remove from the oven and leave to cool.

Meanwhile, heat the oil in a small saucepan over a medium heat. Have a sieve suspended over a heatproof bowl ready to the side. Add the garlic to the pan and fry, stirring once in a while, for about 60–90 seconds, until the garlic is light golden brown. Strain the garlic in the sieve, collecting the oil in the bowl. (You can cool the oil and then transfer it to a jar and keep it in the fridge and use it as garlic oil.) Season the garlic crisps and set aside until needed.

Lay the marrow slices on a baking tray in a single layer. Season them with salt and pepper and drizzle over the dressing or oil. Heat your griddle or chargrill to hot. When hot, cook the marrow slices for 3–4 minutes on each side, until you have good char marks and a smoky flavour (you may need to do this in batches). (When you remove the marrow from the griddle, it should be tender, but if it isn't, place it back on the baking tray and bake it in the oven at 200°C/180°C fan/Gas Mark 6 for 8 minutes, or until tender.)

Transfer the cooked marrow slices to a serving dish, top with the grated cheese, pine nuts, basil and preserved lemon and sprinkle over the fried garlic crisps to serve.

Kalettes are an amazing vegetable, and are a cross between kale and Brussels sprouts. They look rather like a tiny cabbage with green and purple leaves and retain all the goodness of the kale leaf and all the nuttiness of the sprout. So, both healthy and tasty! They are available in the UK from late November to March, so keep an eye out and make the most of them whilst you can. They are great just boiled with salt but the little garnishes in this recipe takes them up a notch or two.

The kalettes, in our opinion, are best boiled then grilled for a nice sweet, smoky flavour. This is a light lunch dish or a great accompaniment for a main meal alongside some grilled fish or meat.

Kalettes
WITH RICOTTA, NIBBED ALMONDS & BURNT HONEY DRESSING

SERVES 4

100g runny honey
50ml chardonnay or other good-
  quality white wine vinegar
50ml rapeseed oil
1 pinch of salt
200g kalettes
100g ricotta
50g nibbed almonds
3 tablespoons salad dressing
  (see page 259) or first-press
  rapeseed oil

Heat the honey in a saucepan over a medium heat for about 2 minutes, until it begins to boil. Boil for about 1 minute, until it starts to darken. Then, add the vinegar, oil and salt and whisk to combine. Remove from the heat and leave to cool. (Once cooled, you can transfer to an airtight container or bottle until needed, if you like, but don't refrigerate, otherwise the dressing will crystallise.)

Heat the griddle or grill to hot. Bring a pan of salted water to the boil. Add the kalettes and boil for about 60 seconds, until just tender with plenty of bite, then drain. Coat the drained kalettes in the dressing or oil, transfer them to the hot griddle or grill and cook for a further 2 minutes, until nicely charred.

To serve, put one quarter of the kalettes on each plate and spoon over the ricotta. Scatter over the almonds and drizzle with the honey dressing.

At Root we love chargrilled vegetables. If you don't have a griddle pan or a grill you can achieve a charred flavour using a very hot frying pan. This simple Asian-inspired broccoli dish can be swapped out for any number of greens and will work just as well. The gochujang mayonnaise is simple to make but you could replace with Tabasco.

Chargrilled tenderstem broccoli
WITH PICKLED GINGER, RED ONION, PEANUT & GOCHUJANG MAYONNAISE

SERVES 4

100g raw peanuts
60g fresh root ginger, peeled and
  thinly sliced into matchsticks
pickle liquid (see page 258)
200g tenderstem broccoli
1 red onion, diced
2 tablespoons salad dressing
  (see page 259) or first-press
  rapeseed oil
dried red onion (optional), to serve
salt and freshly ground
  black pepper

FOR THE MAYONNAISE
35g Dijon mustard
30ml white wine vinegar
3 egg yolks (about 60g)
1 pinch of salt
500ml cooking oil
1 tablespoon gochujang paste
1 tablespoon lemon juice

First, make the mayonnaise. In a food processor or bowl, blend or whisk together the mustard, vinegar, egg yolks and salt. Slowly pour in the oil, blending or whisking all the time until you have used up all the oil. Whisk in the gochujang paste and lemon juice, adding 1 tablespoon of water if the mayonnaise is too thick. Check the seasoning and set aside.

Preheat the oven to 180°C/160°C fan/Gas Mark 4.

Scatter the peanuts over a baking tray and roast for about 15 minutes, giving them a shake halfway through, until evenly coloured all over. Remove from the oven, sprinkle with salt and set aside to cool. When cold, roughly crush and set aside.

Place the ginger in a bowl and pour over the pickle liquid. Set aside.

Heat a griddle or grill pan to hot. Bring a pan of salted water to the boil. Boil the broccoli for about 2 minutes, then drain and coat in the dressing. Transfer the broccoli to the hot griddle or grill pan and cook for a further 2 minutes, until nicely charred. Remove from the heat.

Place the broccoli on a serving dish and scatter over the red onion and drained pickled ginger and the crushed peanuts. Sprinkle over some dried red onion for an extra kick, if you wish. Serve with the mayonnaise on the side. (Store any leftover mayonnaise in an airtight container in the fridge for up to 3 days.)

When Hugh Fearnley-Whittingstall and his wife visited Root and sat at the bar, I spent a fantastic evening cooking and chatting to them both and it was this delicious spiralised swede dish that proved to be their favourite dish of the night. It's one of my favourites as well.

Swede 'tagliatelle'
WITH WILD MUSHROOMS & PICKLED EGG YOLK

SERVES 4

1 swede, peeled
2 tablespoons cooking oil
200g wild mushrooms (such
  as girolles, chanterelles
  or trompettes)
50g salted butter
150ml vegetable stock
100g Parmesan, grated
1 tablespoon lemon juice
1 tablespoon chopped
  flat-leaf parsley
salt and freshly ground
  black pepper

FOR THE PICKLED EGG YOLKS
brine (see page 258)
pickle liquid (see page 258)
4 egg yolks

First, make the pickled egg yolks. Pour the brine and pickle into separate bowls, using enough of each to accommodate the yolks. Pour the yolks into the brine and leave them to soak for 20 minutes, then remove them with a slotted spoon and place them in the bowl with the pickle liquid, leaving them there for 1–2 hours.

When the pickled yolks are ready, make the 'tagliatelle'. Using a spiraliser (the slighter thicker blade if you have a choice), cut the swede into ribbons to resemble tagliatelle. Set aside.

Heat the cooking oil in a frying pan over a high heat. When hot, add the mushrooms and season well with salt and pepper. (You may need to do this in 2 batches – the mushrooms will cook better with fewer in the pan at a time.) Fry for about 1 minute, then (returning the first batch to the pan, if necessary) add the butter and vegetable stock. Bring up to a simmer and add the Parmesan, lemon juice and parsley. Check the seasoning. Keep warm over a low heat.

While the mushrooms are cooking, bring a saucepan of salted water to the boil. Add the swede and cook for 3 minutes, until tender but still retaining a little bite. Transfer to the pan with the mushrooms, and very gently stir to combine, so as not to break up the swede.

Put equal amounts of the hot swede into 4 serving bowls. Pour equal amounts of the mushrooms and sauce over each pile of swede and top with a pickled egg yolk. Finish with a little grinding of black pepper, if you wish.

Carrots simply roasted with honey or agave syrup and some herbs is pretty much carrot heaven. The peaches are a lovely addition, but you could also use apricots, pears or, if you wanted something a little more exotic, kimchi.

Roasted carrots
WITH SPICED PUMPKIN SEEDS, PEACHES & CRÈME FRAÎCHE

SERVES 4

FOR THE SPICED PUMPKIN SEEDS
100g pumpkin seeds
1 pinch of paprika
1 pinch of allspice
1 pinch of ground coriander

FOR THE PICKLED CARROT
1 carrot, peeled and sliced thinly
   with a mandolin
pickle liquid (see page 258)

FOR THE ROASTED CARROTS
2 bunches of carrots (about 16
   carrots), green tops discarded
6 thyme sprigs
6 rosemary sprigs
2 bay leaves
3 garlic cloves, crushed
3 tablespoons runny honey
   or agave syrup
3 tablespoons rapeseed oil
juice of 1 orange
2 peaches, destoned and
   sliced, to serve
100g crème fraîche, to serve
fennel fronds, torn, to garnish
salt and freshly ground
   black pepper

Make the pumpkin seeds. Preheat the oven to 180°C/160°C fan/Gas Mark 4. Scatter the pumpkin seeds over a baking tray and scatter over the spices. Give it all a shake to combine. Place the tray in the oven and roast the seeds for 10–15 minutes, until they are lightly coloured and nicely toasted. Leave to cool, then transfer to a food processor and blitz to a crumb. Set aside.

Make the pickled carrot. Place the thinly sliced carrot in a bowl and pour over pickle liquid to cover. Set aside.

Increase the oven to 200°C/180°C fan/Gas Mark 6.

Make the roasted carrots. We don't peel our carrots, as we feel the softer skin of the variety we use adds to the texture of the dish, but you can peel yours if you prefer. Place the carrots in a baking tray and scatter over the herbs and garlic, and drizzle over the honey or agave and the rapeseed oil. Season well and toss everything together in the tray. Place the tray in the oven and roast the carrots for 15–20 minutes, then add the orange juice to the tray and roast for a further 2 minutes, or until the carrots are tender but retain a good bite (the exact cooking time will depend on the size of your carrots).

Chop the roasted carrots into random sizes and divide them equally among 4 plates. Scatter over the pumpkin-seed crumb, then drizzle over any roasting juices. Add the peach slices and the pickled carrot. Finish with a nice spoonful of crème fraîche and garnish with the fennel fronds.

This is a fantastic autumn dish for when pumpkins and squash are on the shelves. Roasted squash is always delicious, and the nut-free, dairy-free kale pesto is a great match. Try a variety of squash to discover which is your favourite.

Roasted squash
WITH KALE PESTO, SQUASH BARIGOULE PRUNE PURÉE & OLD WINCHESTER

SERVES 4

kale pesto (see page 266)

FOR THE SQUASH BARIGOULE
2 tablespoons cooking oil
1 shallot, sliced
1 carrot, peeled and sliced
1 celery stick, destringed and sliced
1 garlic clove, sliced
1 squash, deseeded and
  thinly sliced
3 thyme sprigs
1 bay leaf
200ml white wine
100ml chardonnay vinegar
500ml vegetable stock
3 tablespoons first-press
  rapeseed oil
80g old Winchester cheese,
  shaved, to serve (optional)

FOR THE ROASTED SQUASH
1 squash, deseeded and cut
  into wedges
3 tablespoons rapeseed oil
3 thyme sprigs, leaves picked
  and chopped
1 rosemary sprig, leaves picked
  and chopped
2 garlic cloves, crushed
1 teaspoon paprika

FOR THE PRUNE PURÉE
200g prunes, pitted
10ml white wine
1 pinch of all spice
1 pinch of salt

For the barigoule, heat the cooking oil in a saucepan over a medium heat. Add the shallot, carrot, celery, and garlic and allow to sweat for 5 minutes, until softened. Add the squash and cook for 3 minutes giving the squash slices a chance to cook a bit. Add the thyme and bay leaf and deglaze the pan with the white wine and vinegar. Add the stock and simmer for 15–18 minutes, until the squash is tender. Check the seasoning. Add the rapeseed oil, then cover and remove from the heat. Allow to cool. Leave the barigoule to mellow for at least 2½ hours, or ideally overnight.

Make the roasted squash. Preheat the oven to 200°C/180°C fan/Gas Mark 6. Scatter the chunks over a baking tray lined with baking paper. Sprinkle over the oil, and scatter over the chopped thyme and rosemary, and the crushed garlic and paprika. Season with a good amount of salt and pepper. Roast in the oven for 12–18 minutes (the kind of squash you use will affect the roasting time), until tender. Check frequently to make sure the squash isn't overcooking. Remove from the oven and set aside.

For the prune purée, place all the ingredients in a saucepan and cover with water. Place the pan over a medium heat and bring to the boil. Boil for 5 minutes, until soft. Remove from the heat and allow to cool slightly, then separate the prunes and liquid, reserving both. Put the prunes into a food processor and blitz, adding the liquid back in until you achieve a smooth purée. You may need to add a little water, too.

To serve, spoon a quarter of the prune purée on to the bottom of each plate. Top with a quarter of the roasted squash, then spoon on top of the squash barigoule and its juices. Drizzle over a little of the pesto (use the remainder for pasta) and sprinkle with the old Winchester cheese to finish, if you wish.

Gazpacho makes for the most wonderfully refreshing start to a meal on a blazing hot day. This was one of the first recipes I ever learnt as a chef. I have it written in a little notebook that I bought over 13 years ago and it is still a favourite. It's very simple to make but so tasty. You can easily scale this recipe up or down the recipe to serve more or fewer people.

Gazpacho
WITH TOASTED SOURDOUGH & VEGETABLE TARTARE

SERVES 8

FOR THE GAZPACHO

1 teaspoon coriander seeds
1 teaspoon cumin seeds
10 plum tomatoes
1 cucumber, peeled
1 red pepper, deseeded
1 green pepper, deseeded
1 red onion
1 garlic clove
10 basil leaves
5 coriander sprigs
1 pinch of cayenne
1 pinch of paprika
500ml tomato juice, plus extra
   if necessary
50ml sherry vinegar
25ml chardonnay vinegar
25ml red wine vinegar
100ml first-press rapeseed oil
2 slices of stale white bread,
   crusts removed, torn
salt and freshly ground
   black pepper

FOR THE VEGETABLE TARTAR

1 green pepper, deseeded and
   cut into 2mm dice
½ cucumber, deseeded and cut
   into 2mm dice
2 tomatoes, deseeded and cut
   into 2mm dice
4 basil leaves, finely shredded
2 tablespoons first-press
   rapeseed oil
1 teaspoon lemon juice

For the gazpacho, first lightly toast the coriander and cumin seeds in a dry frying pan.

Roughly chop the tomatoes, cucumber, peppers, onion and garlic.

Find a large pan or mixing bowl that will fit in your fridge. Add all the gazpacho ingredients and season well with salt and pepper. I like to get my hands dirty, so get stuck in and give everything a good mix and squeeze to help start the marinating process. Cover with cling film and leave in the fridge at least overnight, or even for 2 nights, to allow all the flavours to mingle.

Then, blitz the gazpacho in a food processor, in batches, adding a little more tomato juice or some water to achieve the right consistency – it should be like a soup. Check the seasoning again and refrigerate until you're ready to serve.

For the vegetable tartar, combine the pepper, cucumber and tomatoes in a serving bowl. Add the shredded basil leaves, then stir through the oil and lemon juice. Season to taste with salt and pepper.

Ladle the gazpacho into bowls and top with spoonfuls of the vegetable tartar, serving the rest on the side.

I love the flavour of chargrilled leeks. Root is lucky to have an amazing supplier of locally-grown mushrooms who regularly sends us wonderful shiitake, but you can buy farm-grown shiitake from most supermarkets.

Chargrilled leeks
HAZELNUT 'CREAMED' LEEKS, SAFFRON POTATOES & SHIITAKE MUSHROOMS

SERVES 4

50g hazelnuts
4 leeks, trimmed
1 Maris Piper potato, peeled
    and cut into 1cm dice
1 pinch of saffron strands
4 tablespoons first-press
    rapeseed oil
2 shallots, sliced
1 pinch of salt
1 pinch of paprika
2 tablespoons cooking oil
100g shiitake mushrooms,
    each cut into 4 pieces
1 tablespoon chopped chives

FOR THE HAZELNUT CREAM
100g hazelnuts
20g first-press rapeseed oil, plus
    1 tablespoon for the potatoes

Preheat the oven to 180°C/160°C fan/Gas Mark 4. Place the 50g of hazelnuts on a roasting tray and bake for 15 minutes, or until golden brown. Leave to cool, then crush with the base of a saucepan. Meanwhile heat a griddle or barbecue to hot.

Put 3 of the leeks on the griddle or barbecue grill, turning every 5–6 minutes, until the outsides have blackened and the flesh has softened. Leave to cool, then peel away the outer layers until you are left with 3 beautifully cooked, smoky leeks. Cut each into 4 or 5 pieces and set aside.

Rinse the potatoes and place them in a saucepan of salted water – using just enough water to cover. Add the saffron, place over a medium heat and slowly bring the water to the boil. Once boiling, the potatoes should be tender. Remove from the heat, leave to cool in the cooking water for about 3–5 minutes, then drain. Set aside in the colander while you prepare the hazelnut cream.

Place the hazelnuts, rapeseed oil and 200ml of water in a food processor and blitz until smooth. Set aside until needed.

Cut the remaining leek in half lengthways and thinly slice. Add the rapeseed oil to a large saucepan and place over a low heat. When hot, add the shallots and allow to sweat for 3–5 minutes, until tender, then add the sliced leek and a good pinch of salt. Add a pinch of paprika and cook on a medium–low heat for about 10 minutes, until soft and the excess liquid from the leeks has evaporated. Add the hazelnut cream and cook for a further 5 minutes to warm through, then taste and check the seasoning.

Heat a frying pan over a high heat and add the cooking oil. When hot, add the mushrooms and season well. Fry on a medium–high heat for about 2 minutes, until you have a good colour on all of the mushrooms. Remove from the heat.

To serve, warm the charred leeks in the oven (if necessary), and mix the potatoes with the 1 tablespoon of rapeseed oil and the chopped chives. Spoon the creamed leek mixture on to each plate, top with the charred leeks and dress with the potatoes, mushrooms and hazelnuts.

Mushrooms on toast is one of those classic dishes with which it's best not to meddle. The vegan peppercorn sauce is a good'un, especially soaked up with the toast and the mushrooms.

Mushrooms on toasted focaccia
WITH AN ALMOND & PEPPERCORN SAUCE

SERVES 4

FOR THE PEPPERCORN SAUCE
150g whole almonds, blanched
30ml first-press rapeseed oil
150ml Worcestershire sauce
1 tablespoon green peppercorns
    in brine, drained
1 teaspoon Dijon mustard, plus
    extra to taste if needed
1 teaspoon of caster sugar
1 pinch of cracked black pepper
1 pinch of salt
splash of Tabasco sauce (optional)
splash of brandy (optional), to taste

FOR THE MUSHROOMS
3 tablespoons cooking oil
300g wild or good-quality
    mushrooms
1 teaspoon lemon juice
2 tablespoons chopped
    flat-leaf parsley
1 focaccia (see page 256), to serve

For the peppercorn sauce, put the almonds and rapeseed oil in a food processor with 300ml of water and blitz until smooth. Pass through a sieve into a bowl and set aside.

Put the Worcestershire sauce, peppercorns, mustard, sugar, pepper, salt and Tabasco (if using) in a medium saucepan over a medium heat. Bring to the boil and boil until the liquid has reduced by about four-fifths (about 4–5 minutes).

Add the sieved almond mixture and allow the sauce to come to the boil again. Reduce the heat and simmer for 2 minutes, giving the sauce a good whisk to fully combine. Check the seasoning and add a splash of brandy or a little extra mustard to taste, if necessary. Set aside and keep warm.

If your mushrooms are large, chop them up to bite-sized pieces. Heat the cooking oil in a large frying pan over a high heat. When hot, add the mushrooms and season with a good amount of salt (it's surprising how much salt mushrooms can take). Leave the mushrooms to cook for 30 seconds, then give them a toss in the pan and cook again for a further 30 seconds. Add the lemon juice and chopped parsley. Taste to check the seasoning and make sure the mushrooms are tender, then remove from the heat.

Heat the grill to high, then slice the focaccia into portions. Place the slices on the grill pan and toast under the grill on both sides until golden. (Reheat the peppercorn sauce while you're making the toast, if necessary.)

To serve, spoon the mushrooms on to the focaccia toast and spoon over the hot peppercorn sauce.

When I first discovered just how good a well-roasted shallot was, I began using them in everything! And when used in a tart as here they are just wonderful, whilst the onion purée brings a well-rounded sweetness to it all. The spicy leaves of the cress work perfectly with the sweet caramelised onions.

Caramelised onion & shallot tart
WITH WATERCRESS & PICKLED SHALLOT SALAD

SERVES 4

FOR THE SALAD
2 shallots, very thinly sliced
 into rings
pickle liquid (see page 258)
100g watercress
salad dressing (see page 259)

FOR THE TART
6 banana shallots, skin on
75g caster sugar
3 tablespoons cooking oil
1 x 320g sheet of puff pastry
beaten egg, to glaze
1 recipe quantity of onion purée
 (see page 267)
salt

Preheat the oven to 190°C/170°C fan/Gas Mark 5.

Start the salad. Place the shallot slices in a bowl, sprinkle with a little salt, then add enough pickle liquid to cover. Set aside.

For the tart, trim off the root of the shallots and cut each shallot in half lengthways. Scatter the sugar on to a plate and place the shallots, cut-sides downwards, in the sugar, then transfer them to a clean plate. Set aside.

Heat the cooking oil in a large saucepan over a medium heat. When hot, carefully add the shallots sugared-sides downwards, and cook gently for about 10–12 minutes, until the shallots have a good amount of caramelisation. Add 100ml of water to the pan; this helps deglaze the pan and cook the onions, and intensifies the flavours.

Cook for another 5 minutes. Using 2 forks, carefully turn over each shallot half, turning them skin-sides downwards. Cook for a further 5 minutes, until the shallot halves have softened slightly, then remove from the heat and leave until cool enough to handle.

Meanwhile, lay out the pastry sheet on a baking tray lined with baking paper (or use the paper the pastry comes rolled in) and brush it all over with the egg glaze. Using a sharp knife, score a 2cm border all around the edge of the pastry. Spread the onion purée evenly over the pastry up to the border.

Once the shallot halves are cool enough to handle, remove their skins and place them tightly on top of the purée to cover the tart base. Bake for 20–25 minutes, until the pastry is crisp and golden brown at the edges. (Adjust the temperature during cooking if it looks as though the tart is baking unevenly.)

While the tart is baking, construct the salad. Place the watercress in a serving bowl and scatter over the pickled shallot rings. Drizzle over the dressing. Serve the tart warm, in slices, with the salad alongside.

This is a really good winter dish when greens are in short supply – comforting and delicious and perfect when served with this wholesome yet refreshing cauliflower 'couscous'.

You can make the dhal in advance if you like – it is good served straight away, but I always think dishes like this are even better when you go back to them a few hours later, or even after a few days.

Red lentil dhal
WITH ALMOND & LIME CAULIFLOWER 'COUSCOUS'

SERVES 4–6

FOR THE DHAL
1 teaspoon fennel seeds
1 teaspoon coriander seeds
1 teaspoon cumin seeds
2 tablespoons cooking oil
4 carrots, peeled and diced
4 onions, diced
2 roasted garlic bulbs (see page 267), flesh squeezed out
1 tablespoon onion seeds
1 teaspoon onion powder
1 teaspoon garlic powder
1 teaspoon cayenne pepper
1 teaspoon ground turmeric
1 teaspoon mild curry powder
250g red lentils, rinsed and drained
salt and freshly ground
    black pepper

FOR THE CAULIFLOWER COUSCOUS
75g nibbed or flaked almonds
1 cauliflower, broken into florets
zest and juice of 1 unwaxed lime
2 tablespoons chopped coriander
2 tablespoons pickled mustard seeds (see page 272)
1 tablespoon first-press
    rapeseed oil

Preheat the oven to 190°C/170°C fan/Gas Mark 5.

Place the nibbed or flaked almonds for the cauliflower couscous on one baking tray and the fennel seeds, coriander seeds and cumin seeds for the dhal on another. Roast the almonds for about 12–15 minutes, until golden brown, and the seeds for about 10 minutes, until golden. Remove both from the oven and set aside to cool.

Tip the toasted seeds into a mortar and grind with the pestle until broken up into smaller pieces (or use a food processor, or a spice grinder, if you have one, pulsing until the spices have broken up). Set aside until needed.

Heat the cooking oil in a large saucepan over a medium–high heat. When hot, add the carrots, onions, roasted garlic, onion seeds and onion and garlic powders. Season with salt and pepper, then cook for 5 minutes, adding more oil if the pan looks dry and stirring well, until the vegetables are evenly cooked. Add the toasted, crushed fennel, coriander and cumin seeds and continue to cook for a further 2–3 minutes, then add the cayenne, turmeric, curry powder, red lentils and 1 litre of water. Season again with a good amount of salt and pepper. Bring the mixture to the boil, then lower the heat to a gentle simmer and cook for about 30–40 minutes, until the lentils are soft and the dhal has thickened. Check the seasoning, then remove from the heat.

While the dhal is cooking, make the cauliflower couscous. Place the cauliflower florets and stem into a food processor and blitz briefly, until the cauliflower resembles grains. Don't blend too much, as you will end up with a wet paste rather than something like couscous.

Tip the cauliflower couscous into a mixing bowl and add the toasted almonds, lime zest and juice, chopped coriander, pickled mustard seeds or wholegrain mustard, and rapeseed oil. Season with salt and pepper.

Serve the dhal warm with the cauliflower couscous over the top. Or, if you're making the dhal and couscous as part of a larger meal, serve both separately with more curries and side dishes.

Soft boiled eggs are a joy to eat but crispy soft-boiled hen's eggs are another level. And they are better still with peas and asparagus, giving a little springtime kick. Little girolles are best for pickling as they have a great texture – the larger ones can get bit spongy.

Crispy hen's egg
WITH FRESH PEAS, ASPARAGUS & PICKLED MUSHROOMS

SERVES 4

handful girolle mushrooms or
  punnet of smeji mushrooms
pickle liquid (see page 258)
16 asparagus spears
50g fresh peas
2 tablespoons chopped
  flat-leaf parsley
1 shallot, diced
1 tablespoon lemon juice
2 tablespoons first-press
  rapeseed oil
salt and freshly ground
  black pepper

FOR THE CRISPY EGGS
4 whole eggs, plus 2 beaten eggs
100g plain flour
150g dried breadcrumbs
  (ideally panko)
cooking oil, for frying

Place the mushrooms into a bowl, add a good pinch of salt and pour in pickle liquid to cover. Leave for at least 90 minutes.

While the mushrooms are pickling, make the crispy eggs. Have a bowl of iced water ready to go. Then, bring a medium saucepan of water to the boil. Once boiling, reduce the heat to a simmer and, using a slotted spoon, gently place the whole eggs in the water. Cook the eggs for just over 5 minutes, then remove them from the pan and immediately transfer them to the iced water to cool. Once cooled, carefully peel the eggs and set aside.

Place the flour in one mixing bowl, the beaten egg in a second mixing bowl and the breadcrumbs in a third. Making sure they are well coated at each stage, one by one, dip the boiled eggs into the flour, then into the beaten egg and finally into the breadcrumbs.

Pour the cooking oil into a deep pan until two-thirds full and heat the oil to 180°C on a cooking thermometer or until a cube of day-old bread turns golden in 60 seconds (or preheat a deep-fat fryer to 180°C). Add the coated eggs to the oil and cook for about 1–2 minutes, turning regularly, or until golden brown and crisp. Remove from the oil, drain well and season with a pinch of sea salt. Set aside and keep warm while you make the asparagus.

Using a vegetable peeler, remove the fibrous part from the bases of the asparagus spears to about 2–3cm up the spear. This will leave you with lovely, tender asparagus. Bring a saucepan of salted water to the boil and cook the asparagus for 2–3 minutes, depending on size, until tender. Transfer to a serving tray.

Blanch the peas in the boiling asparagus cooking water for 30 seconds, then drain and transfer to a mixing bowl. Stir through the parsley, shallot, lemon juice and rapeseed oil and season with salt and pepper.

To serve, divide the asparagus spears equally among 4 plates and top each serving with a crispy-coated egg. Scatter the pea mixture around the edge and finish with a good few drained pickled mushrooms.

Why don't we eat more pulses! They are versatile, delicious and also happen to be an important part of a healthy and balanced diet. When we started making our own crème fraîche at Root we found ourselves tempted to add it to all and everything. We calmed down after a while. But I have to say that finishing this dish with a couple of spoonfuls of crème fraîche really raises the dish to the next level, giving a dash of sourness and piquancy. Choose chunky courgettes so that you can get a good charring and buy fresh large-leaf spinach to give body.

Roasted courgettes
WITH PUY LENTILS, SPINACH & CRÈME FRAÎCHE

SERVES 4

FOR THE LENTILS

300g puy lentils, soaked overnight or for at least 1 hour
900ml vegetable stock
200ml red wine
3 rosemary sprigs
3 thyme sprigs
2 garlic cloves, crushed
1 bay leaf
2 tablespoons cooking oil
1 carrot, peeled and chopped into small dice
2 celery sticks, destringed and chopped into small dice
1 handful of spinach
4 tablespoons crème fraîche
4 tablespoons chopped parsley
salt and freshly ground black pepper

FOR THE COURGETTES

4 small courgettes, halved lengthways
3 tablespoons cooking oil
1 tablespoon lemon juice

Drain and rinse the soaked lentils. Pour the vegetable stock and red wine into a saucepan and place over a medium heat. Season with salt and pepper and add the rosemary, thyme, garlic and bay leaf. Bring to a simmer and cook gently for about 15–20 minutes, until the lentils are tender but still retain a little bite.

While the lentils are cooking, heat the cooking oil in a medium saucepan over a high heat. Add the carrot and celery and season with salt and pepper. Fry for about 90 seconds, until they are tender but with plenty of bite. Once the lentils are cooked, add the carrot and celery mixture to the pan.

Towards the end of the lentil cooking time, make the courgettes. Turn the courgettes cut-sides upwards. Using a sharp knife, score the flesh with a criss-cross pattern and season well.

Heat the 3 tablespoons of cooking oil in a large frying pan over a medium heat. Add the courgettes, scored-sides downwards, and cook for 4–5 minutes, until the cut sides have taken on some really nice colour. Turn the courgettes over and cook the other sides for a further 5 minutes, until coloured. Sprinkle the lemon juice over the courgettes and remove from the heat.

Stir the spinach into the hot lentil mixture, along with the crème fraîche and chopped parsley. Ladle the lentils equally into serving bowls and top proudly with the courgette halves.

This courgette ragù is a favourite staff lunch at Root – it's quick to prepare, packed full of flavour and quite delicious. We often cook it in a marrow, as here, but it's also a joy with fish, meat and pasta.

Courgette ragù
BAKED IN A MARROW

SERVES 4

FOR THE MARROW
1 large or 2 small marrows
4 tablespoons rapeseed oil
2 thyme sprigs, leaves picked
salt and freshly ground
    black pepper

FOR THE COURGETTE RAGÙ
2 tablespoons cooking oil
3 shallots, diced
2 garlic cloves, minced
1 roasted garlic bulb (see page
    267), flesh squeezed out
4 courgettes, cut into 2cm dice
250ml white wine
250ml vegetable stock
100ml double cream
100g Parmesan or other hard
    cheese, grated, plus an extra
    50g for sprinkling
2 tablespoons chopped chives
2 tablespoons chopped parsley
1 tablespoon lemon juice
salt

Preheat the oven to 200°C/180°C fan/Gas Mark 6.

Cut the marrow(s) in half lengthways and, using a spoon, scrape out the seeds and any pulp (you're aiming to leave a good hollow for the ragù). Score the flesh slightly and brush the rapeseed oil over. Season well with salt and pepper and scatter over the thyme leaves. Place the marrow halves on a baking tray lined with baking paper and bake for 10 minutes, until tender but still holding their shape. Remove from the oven and set aside until needed.

Make the ragù. Heat the cooking oil in a large saucepan over a medium heat. Add the diced shallots and both garlics. Allow to sweat for 5 minutes, stirring occasionally, until softened.

Add the courgettes to the pan with a good seasoning of salt and turn up the heat. Cook, stirring often, for 5 minutes, or until you have a good amount of colour on the courgettes, then add the white wine. Reduce the heat to a gentle simmer and cook until the liquid has reduced by two-thirds. Then, add the stock and simmer for a further 5 minutes, until reduced again by one-third. Add the cream and the cheese and cook for 10 minutes on a low heat, until thick and sauce-y (almost like a pie filling). Finally, add the herbs and lemon juice and season to taste.

Spoon the ragù equally into the marrow halves and sprinkle with the remaining 50g of grated cheese. Bake for 10 minutes, until the cheese is melted and golden and the ragù is bubbling, then serve straight away.

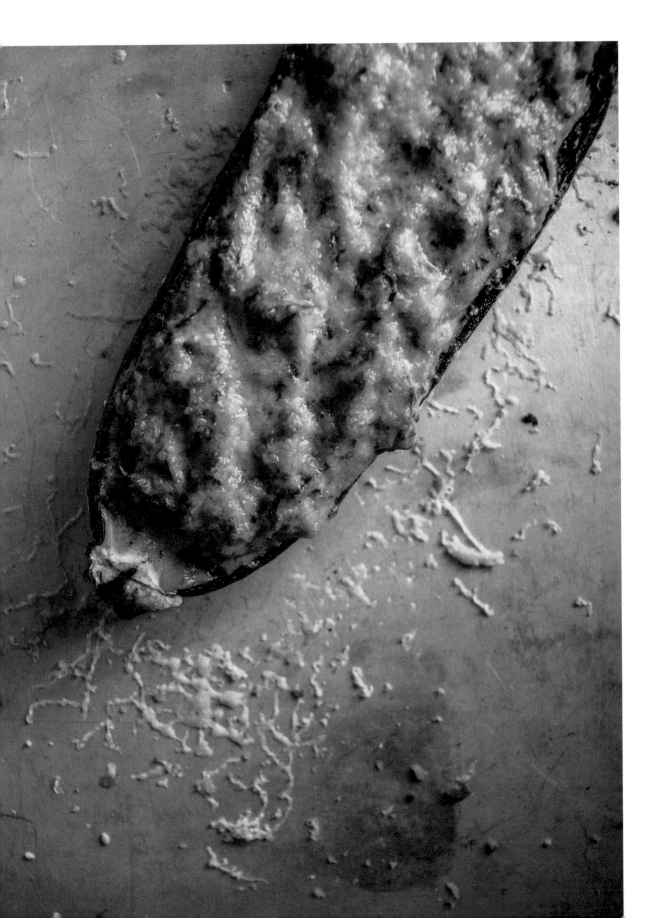

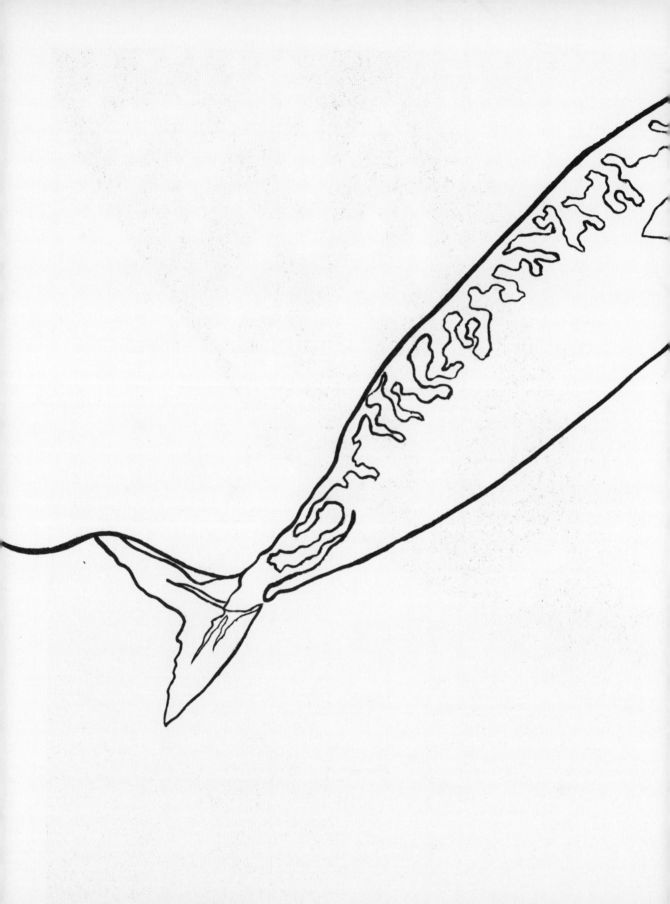

meat & fish

You always remember your first oyster! I was 16 years old and doing a chef stage at Nathan Outlaw's 2 Michelin star fish restaurant in Rock. It was early in the morning! Whilst eating the staff porridge I told one of the chefs that I had never tried an oyster, so rising to the challenge he swiftly shucked a fresh Porthilly oyster for me to try there and then. And so it was that I was inducted into the art of eating and enjoying oysters.

A crispy oyster is what I would regard as a beginner's oyster – a good entry level introduction from which you can work your way up to the fresh. Once you get the oyster habit I can guarantee that you won't stop searching them out on menus, enjoying discovering the many varieties with all their subtle differences in flavour and texture.

Oysters two ways
FRESH OYSTER WITH CHILLI, GINGER & GHERKIN / CRISPY OYSTER WITH TARTARE SAUCE

SERVES 4

8 oysters

FOR THE CHILLI DRESSING
1 gherkin, cut into 2mm dice, plus 50ml of the juice in the jar
6cm piece of fresh ginger root, peeled and cut into 2mm dice
1 garlic clove, finely chopped
1 shallot, cut into 2mm dice
1 red chilli, deseeded and cut into 2mm dice
50ml pickle liquid (see page 258)

FOR THE CRISPY OYSTERS
100g plain flour
2 eggs, beaten
150g dried breadcrumbs (use panko, if possible)
cooking oil, for deep frying
sea salt

FOR THE TARTARE SAUCE
3 egg yolks (about 60g)
30ml white wine vinegar
1 pinch of salt

Prepare the chilli dressing for the fresh oysters at least 1 hour before you intend to serve. Place all the ingredients in a bowl, covering with the gherkin juice and pickle liquid. Leave for 1 hour – this will help to soften the vegetables.

Prepare the crispy oysters ready to fry. Carefully open 4 of the oysters using an oyster knife (you'll need an oyster knife, rather than a standard knife), making sure there is no shell attached. Keep the shells and wash them (you can serve your crispy oysters in them).

Place the flour in one bowl, the beaten egg in a second bowl and the breadcrumbs in a third. Making sure the oysters are well coated at each stage, one by one, dip the oysters into the flour, then into the beaten egg and finally into the breadcrumbs, gently shaking off any excess. Set aside on a plate and refrigerate while you make the tartare sauce. (You can do this in advance and leave refrigerated, covered, for up to 1 day, if you prefer.)

To make the tartare sauce, combine the yolks, vinegar, salt and mustard in a bowl and whisk together. Slowly add the rapeseed oil, whisking all the time, until the mixture comes together and all the oil has been incorporated. (It's easier if you have someone to hold the bowl for you; or use an electric stand mixer or food processor.) Whisk in the lemon juice, capers, chopped gherkins or cornichons and herbs. Season to taste.

Shuck the remaining 4 oysters, clean the shells and put the oysters back inside. Place them in a dish on a bed of wet salt or crushed ice. Refrigerate until ready to serve.

35g Dijon mustard
500ml rapeseed oil
1 tablespoon lemon juice
2 tablespoons capers
2 tablespoons finely chopped
 gherkins (or use
 chopped cornichons)
2 tablespoons chopped chives
2 tablespoons chopped
 flat-leaf parsley
salt and freshly ground
 black pepper

When you're ready to construct the dish, pour the cooking oil into a deep pan until two-thirds full and heat to 180°C on a cooking thermometer or until a cube of day-old bread turns golden in 60 seconds (or preheat a deep-fat fryer to 180°C). Remove the coated oysters from the fridge and deep fry for about 1 minute, turning frequently, until golden brown and crisp all over. Remove from the oil, drain well on a piece of kitchen paper and season with sea salt.

Spoon a dollop of tartare sauce into each shell and top each with a crispy oyster. Remove the fresh oysters from the fridge and spoon a good amount of chilli dressing into each. Serve everything immediately.

I love this dish – easy to prepare and to cook, producing the most wonderfully fresh and tasty result.

For me fresh mackerel is up there with the best that the ocean can offer – just make sure that you get the freshest fish possible. Salt the fish's flesh well before cooking as this will give a lovely translucence to the mackerel. The oiliness of the mackerel paired with the freshness of the cucumber and the apple takes a little heat away from the fiery jalapeno mayonnaise.

Grilled mackerel
WITH CUCUMBER, APPLE & MINT SALSA & JALAPEÑO MAYONNAISE

SERVES 4

4 skin-on mackerel fillets,
    pin boned
2 tablespoons rapeseed oil,
    for brushing

FOR THE JALAPEÑO MAYONNAISE

35g Dijon mustard
30g white wine vinegar
3 egg yolks (about 60g)
12 jalapeño chillies, deseeded
    and finely chopped
1 pinch of sea salt
500ml cooking oil
1 tablespoon of lemon juice

FOR THE SALSA

2 Granny Smith apples, peeled,
    cored and cut into 1cm dice
1 cucumber, deseeded and cut
    into 1cm dice
12 mint leaves, sliced into ribbons
3 tablespoons chive oil (see page
    268), or use rapeseed oil
1 teaspoon lemon juice
1 pinch of sea salt, plus extra
    to season

Prepare the mackerel fillets 30 minutes before you intend to cook. Make sure there are no stray bones, then make shallow cuts through the skin side, just into the flesh. Turn over each fillet and season with sea salt (just as you would a steak). Place in the fridge for 30 minutes to cure slightly – the fillets will firm up and let out some of their liquid.

While the fillets are curing, make the mayonnaise and salsa.

For the mayonnaise, put the mustard, vinegar, egg yolks, jalapeños and salt into a bowl and whisk to combine. Slowly pour in the oil, whisking the whole time, until you have incorporated all the oil (you may find it easier if someone else holds the bowl for you; or use an electric stand mixer or food processor). Whisk in the lemon juice and check the seasoning. Add a tablespoon of water if the mayonnaise is too thick. Set aside.

For the salsa, combine the apple and cucumber in a bowl. Add the mint, along with the oil, lemon juice and salt. Stir gently to combine and set aside.

When the fillets are ready, heat the grill to medium–high.

Line a baking tray with 4 fillet-sized pieces of baking paper. Brush both sides of the fillets with oil and sprinkle the skin with a little sea salt. Place the fillets in the baking tray, each on top of a piece of baking paper, skin-sides downwards. Grill for 3–4 minutes, or until the fish is just cooked – the skin should be nicely blistered and slightly crispy. Remove from the grill and place each fillet on to a serving plate with a good dollops of mayonnaise and salsa on the side.

I'd guess that nowadays most people's introduction to squid is calamari with sweet chilli sauce. This dish has the same flavour profiles; the sweet jam pairs with the gentle heat and acid from the pickled chilli to hit all the spots. Cooking squid may seem daunting but it's actually super quick and easy – two minutes in a hot pan and its done.

Pan-fried squid
WITH PICKLED CHILLI, PEANUT CRUMB & CARROT JAM

SERVES 4

600g prepared squid, bodies
   and tentacles separated
4 tablespoons cooking oil
1 tablespoon lemon juice
½ bunch of coriander, chopped
salt and freshly ground
   black pepper

FOR THE PICKLED CHILLIES
2 red chillies, halved, deseeded
   and thinly sliced
pickle liquid (see page 258)
salt

FOR THE CARROT JAM
300g carrots, peeled and sliced
200ml carrot juice
180g caster sugar

FOR THE PEANUT CRUMB
200g raw peanuts
1 pinch of allspice
1 pinch of ground coriander
1 pinch of sea salt

At least 30 minutes before you intend to serve, make the pickled chillies, which need at least 30 minutes before using (you can make them well in advance and store them in the fridge, if you like). Place the chilli slices in a bowl, sprinkle with a little salt and cover with pickle liquid. Leave for at least 30 minutes.

For the carrot jam, put all the ingredients in a saucepan with 300ml of water and place over a medium heat. Bring to the boil, then reduce the heat and simmer for about 15–20 minutes, until the carrots are tender and mixture looks jammy. Leave to cool slightly, then place in a food processor and blitz well until you have a smooth purée. (Add a little extra water if it's too thick to blend well.) Transfer the jam to a jar or other container and leave to cool. Set aside until you're ready to serve. (If you don't use all the jam, it will keep in the fridge for about 2 weeks.)

While the jam is simmering, make the peanut crumb. Preheat the oven to 180°C/160°C fan/Gas Mark 4. Scatter the peanuts over a baking tray and roast for 14–18 minutes, checking the peanuts halfway through cooking and giving them a shake to ensure an even roast, until golden brown. Remove from the oven and allow to cool. Once cool, place the peanuts, spices and salt into a blender and blitz to a fine crumb (take care not to overwork the nuts, or you'll end up with paste). Set aside.

Halve the squid bodies and score the inside flesh with a criss-cross pattern (this will help them to cook evenly). Slice the bodies into ribbons roughly of the same size, and then cut the tentacles into similarly sized pieces. Season all the squid with salt and a nice amount of black pepper.

Heat the oil in a large saucepan on a high heat. When hot, add the squid, making sure each piece is in contact with the pan (cook in 2 batches, if necessary). Cook the squid for 1 minute on one side and turn it over and cook it for another 30 seconds on the other, until golden, then add the lemon juice. Give the pan a good shake and remove from the heat. Sprinkle over the coriander and transfer the squid to a serving plate for people to help themselves. Finish with dots of carrot jam, a sprinkle of peanut crumb and a few pickled chillies.

Taramasalata is an always popular Greek dip that I serve with fresh, peppery radishes. It's just as good at the start of a meal though with perhaps a selection of vegetable crudités or freshly baked bread or both.

If you're not a fan of radishes, you can use any fresh, crunchy vegetables for dipping.

Smoked cod's roe dip
SERVED WITH FRESH RADISHES

SERVES 4

180g smoked cod's roe, skin removed
1 roasted garlic bulb (see page 267), flesh squeezed out
1 pinch of paprika
1 pinch of cayenne pepper
1 teaspoon Dijon mustard
250ml cooking oil
2 tablespoons lemon juice
2 tablespoons sherry vinegar
2 tablespoons rapeseed oil
2 bunches of radishes, green tops intact, for dipping

Place the skinless cod's roe in a food processor with the roasted garlic and the paprika, cayenne and mustard. Blitz to a smooth paste. Scrape down the sides of the processor bowl, replace the lid and turn the processor to high speed. Slowly begin to add the cooking oil through the feed tube. Once the mixture thickens, add 100ml of water, then add the remaining oil. Finally, add the lemon juice and sherry vinegar. The dip should be smooth and thick, like the consistency of whipped cream. If it's too thick, add some water; if it's too thin, add a little more oil.

Transfer the dip to a serving bowl and drizzle with the rapeseed oil. Serve with the radishes alongside for dipping. (You can make the dip up to 5 days in advance, if you store it in an airtight container in the fridge.)

Simple is usually best with great produce. And crab is great! This dish went on the Root menu after I went to a food festival and had a delicious plate of crab and chips – it was the best thing I had eaten in months. I took the inspiration back home and here's my own little version.

You can make the crab in advance but it is best eaten as fresh as possible. If you make it in advance, you can keep it covered in the fridge, for up to 2 days.

Dressed crab
WITH SPRING ONIONS & CONFIT POTATOES

SERVES 4

300g picked white crab meat
2 tablespoons mayonnaise
   (see page 266)
1 tablespoon chopped chives
1 tablespoon lemon juice
1 pinch of paprika
4 spring onions, finely sliced,
   to serve
salt and freshly ground
   black pepper

FOR THE CONFIT POTATOES
a handful of new potatoes,
   cut into 5mm slices
2 thyme sprigs
2 bay leaves
2 garlic cloves, crushed
about 500ml cooking oil

Using a spoon, in a bowl carefully combine the crab meat with the mayonnaise, chives, lemon juice and paprika. Season with salt and a little black pepper. (Try to be gentle as the meat will break down and make the texture too paste-like if you over-mix.) Set aside, covered, while you cook the potatoes.

Place the potato slices in a large saucepan – add them in layers, if you can, seasoning with salt and pepper and adding torn pieces of the herbs and a little garlic between the layers. Pour in enough oil to just cover the sliced potatoes and lay a sheet of baking paper over the top. Place the pan over a low–medium heat and slowly bring to a gentle simmer. Cook the potatoes for about 10–15 minutes, until tender but still holding their shape.

We have served it back in the crab shells for a bit more theatre, but if you don't have the shells then it's not a problem. Remove the potatoes from the excess oil. Divide the potatoes equally among 4 crab shells or over 4 plates. Spoon equal amounts of the crab on top and finish with a sprinkling of spring onion. Serve immediately.

This fantastic Asian-inspired dish is one of my all-time favourites. The large amount of roasted garlic goes towards adding a delicious and essential hit of garlicky sweetness.

Baked seaweed hake
WITH TIKKA MASALA-STYLE SAUCE & BOK CHOI

SERVES 4

4 heads of bok choi, quartered
4 hake fillets (each about 200g)
40g unsalted butter,
    cut into 4 slices
5g seaweed flakes
2 tablespoons rapeseed oil
1 teaspoon lemon juice
2 tablespoons chopped coriander
salt

FOR THE TIKKA SAUCE
10 shallots
4 garlic bulbs
5 tomatoes
3 tablespoons cooking oil,
    plus extra if needed
1 red chilli, sliced
6cm piece of fresh root ginger,
    peeled and chopped
1 tablespoon tomato purée
2 tablespoons caster sugar
2 tablespoons ground cumin
3 tablespoons mild curry powder
1 tablespoon paprika
2 tablespoons garam masala
1 teaspoon chilli powder
1 teaspoon turmeric
1 litre vegetable stock
salt and freshly ground
    black pepper

Preheat the oven to 170°C/150°C fan/Gas Mark 3.

Start by making the tikka sauce. Lay the shallots in a baking tray in their skins. Lay the garlic and tomatoes in a separate baking tray. Roast the shallots for 50–60 minutes and the garlic and tomatoes for 30–40 minutes, until soft. Remove both trays from the oven and leave everything to cool. When cool, cut the tops off the shallots and squeeze out the soft, roasted flesh into a bowl and roughly chop it up. Repeat with the garlic. Leave the roasted tomatoes to the side.

Heat the cooking oil in a large saucepan over a medium heat. Add the chopped roasted shallots and garlic, along with the sliced chilli and the ginger. Season with salt and cook for 5 minutes, then add the tomato purée, sugar and spices. Add more oil, if the pan is dry, and stir well, cooking for a further 2 minutes, to cook out the spices. Add the roasted tomatoes (skin on) and the vegetable stock. Bring to a gentle simmer, then simmer for 20 minutes, until the shallots are tender. Remove from the heat and leave to cool slightly. Blitz in a food processor to a smooth sauce and check the seasoning. Keep warm.

Place a saucepan of salted water over a high heat and bring to the boil. Add the bok choi quarters and cook for 60 seconds, until slightly softened. Remove from the heat and drain.

Preheat the oven to 200°C/180°C fan/Gas Mark 6.

Season the hake on both sides with salt and place the fillets skin sides upwards on a lined baking tray. Place a slice of butter on the top of each fillet and sprinkle with seaweed flakes. Bake for 5 minutes, until the flesh is opaque and the fish is cooked through. Remove from the oven and set aside. Keep warm.

Heat the 2 tablespoons of rapeseed oil in a frying pan over a high heat. When hot, add the bok choi and season with salt. Fry for 2 minutes (you may need to do this in batches), until there is a good amount of colour on the bok choi, then sprinkle over the lemon juice and coriander.

To serve, divide the bok choi equally among 4 bowls. Spoon the sauce on the side and place a fillet of hake on top.

Sardine Bolognese? Perhaps not the most appetising sounding of dishes and I was certainly pretty sceptical when Josh Eggleton first sang its praises. But once tasted I was converted and sardine bolognese is now one of my favourite things to eat either with pasta, rice or on toast. Try it and be amazed!

You can cook the bolognese in advance and either freeze it or refrigerate it for 3–5 days before serving. If anything, it gets better if it's left overnight.

Josh's sardine bolognaise on toast

SERVES 6

15 fresh sardines, butterflied
2 tablespoons cooking oil
2 celery sticks, destringed and cut into 1cm pieces
2 shallots, cut into 1cm dice
1 carrot, peeled and cut into 1cm dice
1 fennel, cut into 1cm dice
1 garlic clove, minced
1 roasted garlic bulb (see page 267), flesh squeezed out
1 tablespoon tomato purée
1 pinch of paprika
1 pinch of white pepper
1 bay leaf
4 thyme sprigs
1 tablespoon plain flour
200ml red wine
1 x 400g tin of chopped tomatoes
200ml shop-bought, reduced fresh beef stock (or make up with a stock cube)
25ml Worcestershire sauce
25ml sherry vinegar
zest and juice of 1 lemon
6 slices of bread, toasted and buttered, to serve
salt

Remove the tail and the top fin of the sardines. Pulse the fish in a food processor until they combine to look like sausagemeat. Set aside until needed.

Heat the oil in a large saucepan on a medium–high heat. When hot, add the celery, shallots, carrot, fennel and both garlics. Stir well and season with a good amount of salt, then cook for about 2–3 minutes, or until the vegetables start to take on a nice, golden colour.

Add the tomato purée, paprika, white pepper, bay and thyme and continue to cook, adding a little oil to prevent the mixture catching at the bottom of the pan. Cook for 2 minutes, then add the blitzed sardines and cook, stirring well, for about 2 minutes, until the fish takes on some colour. After a further 2–3 minutes, add the tablespoon of flour and cook out for 2–3 minutes. Pour in the red wine and simmer for about 2 minutes, stirring well, until the liquid has reduced to almost nothing. Add the tinned tomatoes, beef stock, Worcestershire sauce and vinegar and lower the heat. Cook for a good 30–40 minutes, or until the sauce has the consistency of a meaty bolognese. Add the lemon zest and juice, and adjust the seasoning, if necessary.

Lay out a piece of well-buttered toast on each plate, then serve topped with lashings of the bolognese.

If you are fortunate enough to have very fresh fish to hand, serving it ceviche style is a great way to make the most of it. The cure helps firm the flesh giving it a great texture once 'cooked' in the lime juice.

Cured sea bream
WITH PICKLED CHILLI, CUCUMBER, CAPER & RAISIN PURÉE & DILL OIL

SERVES 4

60g sea salt
40g caster sugar
zest of 1 lime and juice of 2
4 skinless, boneless sea bream
   fillets (each about 120g)
dill oil (see page 268)

FOR THE CAPER AND RAISIN PURÉE
500g raisins
2 tablespoons capers
salt

FOR THE PICKLES
2 red chillies, deseeded and sliced
½ cucumber, sliced into
   2mm rounds
1 tablespoon chopped dill
pickle liquid (see page 258)
salt

Make a cure for the fish. Combine the salt, sugar and lime zest in a mixing bowl. One by one, coat each fillet in the cure. Place the coated fillets on a tray or plate and refrigerate for 80–90 minutes. Then, remove from the fridge, rinse off the cure in a bowl of cold water and pat the fillets dry. Return the fillets to the fridge until you're ready to serve.

While the fillets are in the cure, make the purée. Tip the raisins and capers into a saucepan and cover with water. Place the pan over a high heat and bring to a simmer. Simmer for 10 minutes, until softened, then drain, reserving the cooking liquid. Transfer the raisins and capers to a blender and blitz with a small amount of the cooking liquid until you have a smooth purée. Season with salt and refrigerate until needed.

To make the pickles, place the chilli slices in one bowl and the cucumber slices and dill in another. Sprinkle a good amount of salt into each bowl, then cover the cucumber and chilli slices with pickle liquid.

To serve, slice the sea bream fillets on an angle into thin slices. Arrange the slices on a serving platter and sprinkle over the lime juice and dill oil. Dot the purée over the fish and finish with a scattering of pickled chilli and pickled cucumber. Serve immediately, before the fish has time to 'cook' in the lime juice (which will affect the texture).

We like to use sardines whenever we can at the restaurant – they are always in good supply, cheap and very tasty. We get a small amount daily off the boats to use the same day – with sardines freshness is the key. Sardines simply grilled with lemon juice are great but this kimchi gives a fabulous added extra hit of flavour. Ask your fishmonger to butterfly the sardines for you.

Grilled butterflied sardines
WITH KIMCHI-STYLE CABBAGE

SERVES 4

8 sardines, butterflied
3 tablespoons first-press
    rapeseed oil
3 tablespoons lemon juice
salt

FOR THE KIMCHI -STYLE CABBAGE
1 head of Chinese leaf, sliced
2 per cent of the weight of the
    sliced leaves in sea salt
100g gochujang paste

First, make the kimchi. Put the sliced leaf in a large tray or bowl. Add the salt, massaging it into the leaf, squeezing to release the juice. Keep going until you have enough juice to cover the shredded leaves. Add the gochujang paste and mix well.

Transfer the mixture to a bowl or container and cover with baking paper. Sit another bowl or container on top of the baking paper to press down, ensuring the shredded leaves are submerged in juice. Leave in a cool, dry place (somewhere at 18°–23°C is ideal) for 5 days, until the leaf has fermented. Transfer to an airtight container and refrigerate until needed.

Preheat a grill or chargrill to hot. Brush the sardines with the rapeseed oil and season with salt on both sides. Cook, skin-sides downwards, on a piece of baking paper in a hot pan or on a grill pan for about 90 seconds, until the skin is crisp and the flesh just cooked.

Place 2 sardines on each plate and drizzle with a little of the lemon juice. Season with salt, if needed, and serve with the kimchi alongside.

Monkfish, the ugly fish with an inner beauty, is amazing to cook and very versatile. The meatiness of the flesh means it can withstand a serious amount of flavour. It's best to be cooked on the bone, or in large pieces, and then left to rest to ensure a deliciously juicy result. Here the sides are a perfect flavourful match for the spiced monkfish.

Spiced monkfish
WITH CURRIED ONIONS, APPLE SAUCE, MINT & CORIANDER YOGHURT

SERVES 4

30g sea salt, plus extra to season and for the other elements
20g caster sugar
500g skinless monkfish on the bone, sinew removed
1 tablespoon mild curry powder
1 tablespoon turmeric
1 teaspoon paprika
1 teaspoon ground coriander
1 teaspoon cayenne pepper
50g unsalted butter

FOR THE CURRIED ONIONS
2 tablespoons first-press rapeseed oil
3 onions, sliced
1 teaspoon mild curry powder
1 teaspoon cayenne pepper

FOR THE APPLE SAUCE
4 cooking apples, peeled
50ml sherry vinegar

FOR THE SEASONED YOGHURT
300g natural yoghurt
4 tablespoons chopped coriander
1 tablespoon chopped mint

Combine the salt and sugar in a bowl and use to season the fish. Place the fish on a plate, cover and leave in the fridge for 45–60 minutes to cure.

While the fish is curing, prepare the other elements. First, make the curried onions. Heat the rapeseed oil in a medium saucepan over a medium heat. When warm, add the sliced onions and season with a good amount of salt. Add the curry powder and cayenne pepper and allow to cook on a medium–low heat, stirring occasionally, for at least 20–25 minutes, until soft and sweet. (The longer the cooking time, the better flavour and texture.) Taste frequently to check the seasoning, and add more oil if the pan is dry.

Meanwhile, make the apple sauce. Core and roughly chop 3 of the apples and put them in a medium saucepan over a medium–high heat. Add the vinegar and a pinch of salt and cook for 5 minutes, stirring often to stop them catching as they soften, until completely soft and golden brown (I prefer a nice amount of colour to my apple sauce). Leave to cool slightly, then transfer to a food processor and blitz to a purée. Add the purée back into the pan. Core, then cut the remaining apple into small dice. Add the dice to the pan and place over a medium heat. Cook for 3–4 minutes, until the diced apple has slightly softened. Set aside.

Make the seasoned yoghurt by combining the yoghurt, coriander, mint and a pinch of sea salt in a bowl. Set aside.

Once the monkfish has cured, remove from the fridge, rinse it and pat dry. Mix the spices together in a bowl and spread them out over a clean baking tray. Roll the monkfish in the spices, making sure it's covered all over, then pat it with kitchen paper to remove any excess spices. Set aside for 10 minutes to come up in temperature a bit and preheat the oven to 220°C/200°C fan/Gas Mark 7.

Add a little cooking oil to a frying pan over a medim heat. Gently place the monkfish in the pan and colour on each side for 2 minutes before placing on a lined baking tray. Dot the butter over the top, then bake the fish for 10-12 minutes, or until the flesh almost pulls away from the bone indicating it's cooked. Allow to rest for 5 minutes, then serve the fish in a single portion with the minty yoghurt, apple sauce and curried onions alongside, for everyone to help themselves.

Not only is brandade an amazing dish but it is also a fantastic way to use up trimmings and odds and ends – a great example of the whole fish philosophy in practice. In the restaurant, when portioning fish, there are always parts that don't quite make the cut so we like to save all of those parts for later use. I've suggested cod here but the recipe would work just as well with any white fish, so try to get into the habit of remembering to ask your fishmonger for off cuts – they go a long way.

Cod brandade
WITH SOURDOUGH TOAST

SERVES 6

3 large Maris Piper potatoes,
    peeled and cut into 4cm pieces
500g boneless cod offcuts
500ml whole milk
3 garlic cloves, 2 crushed, 1 minced
2 bay leaves
5 peppercorns
2 thyme sprigs
150ml first-press rapeseed oil
2 large or 4 small shallots, diced
1 teaspoon paprika
1 teaspoon curry powder
1 tablespoon lemon juice
1 tablespoon chopped chives
1 tablespoon chopped parsley
1 teaspoon Dijon mustard
slices of sourdough bread,
    toasted, to serve
salt and freshly ground
    black pepper

Place the potatoes in a medium saucepan and place under running water until the water runs clear (this drains off the starch). Cover the potatoes with water and place the pan on a medium heat. Bring to a simmer and cook for about 15 minutes, until the potatoes are soft. Drain and leave in the colander to dry.

While the potatoes are cooking, place the fish and milk in a saucepan with the crushed garlic, and the bay, peppercorns and thyme. Place over a medium heat and bring to a simmer (about 5 minutes). As soon as the mixture starts to simmer, remove from the heat and cover the pan, leaving the fish to poach in the residual heat for about 6 minutes, until cooked through. Drain and reserve the poaching liquid and set this and the fish aside.

Heat the oil in a saucepan over a medium heat. When hot, add the shallots, the minced garlic, and the paprika, curry powder and a good seasoning of salt. Cook on a low–medium heat for 5 minutes to almost confit the shallots and cook out the spices.

Tip the potatoes into a large mixing bowl and crush using a masher or your hands. Add the shallots, along with their cooking oil, and the fish. Add a little of the poaching liquid to loosen the mixture to a nice, spreadable consistency, then mix in the lemon juice, chopped herbs and the mustard. Check the seasoning and serve hot with toasted sourdough.

This is a dressing that I first made when working at Goodfellows restaurant in Wells 13 years ago. It goes to show that some cooking is resistant to fashion and can stand the test of time. It is simple and tasty and pairs perfectly with a nice chunky piece of cod which stands up well to the smoky pancetta flavour of the dressing. It's also great with waxy new potatoes.

Roast cod
WITH GEM LETTUCE & PANCETTA & HAZELNUT DRESSING

SERVES 4

4 skinless, boneless cod fillets
    (about 120g each)
40g unsalted butter
2 tablespoons cooking oil
4 baby gems, halved
sea salt and freshly ground
    black pepper

FOR THE PANCETTA DRESSING
100ml first-press rapeseed oil
250g smoked pancetta, cut into
    about 1cm dice
2 red onions, finely diced
150ml red wine
50ml sherry vinegar
50g roasted and crushed hazelnuts
    (see page 138)

Salt the cod flesh lightly with sea salt and leave in the fridge until needed.

Make the dressing. Heat 1 tablespoon of the rapeseed oil in a medium saucepan on a low heat. Add the diced pancetta, increase the heat to medium and cook, stirring well, for about 15–20 minutes, until perfectly crisp. Remove from the heat and scoop out the meat using a slotted spoon. Set aside.

Put the pan (including the rendered fat) back on the heat and add the onions. Cook on a medium–high heat for about 5 minutes, stirring well, until soft. Add the red wine and sherry vinegar and cook for about 2 minutes, until the liquid has reduced by two-thirds. Add the meat back to the pan, along with the crushed hazelnuts and the remaining rapeseed oil. Mix well, taste and adjust the seasoning, if necessary. Set aside.

Preheat the oven to 200°C/180°C fan/Gas Mark 6.

Place the cod on a baking tray lined with baking paper. Dot the butter all over the fish and bake for about 5–6 minutes, until just cooked and translucent.

Meanwhile, heat the oil in a frying pan over a high heat. Season the baby gem halves and add them to the pan, cooking for 2 minutes, turning, until coloured all over, but still with good texture.

To serve, place 2 baby gem halves on each plate and top each serving with a cod fillet. Finish with lashings of the dressing, making sure everyone gets good amounts of the pancetta and hazelnuts.

Scallops are delicious either raw or cooked. If serving scallops raw make sure you use the best quality scallops and that they are as fresh as possible. I've used elderberry vinegar in this recipe, but it would work just as well with other flavoured vinegars or indeed citrus juice. Make sure to cook the scallops briefly and never overcook as they can turn rubbery very quickly.

Scallops two ways

RAW SCALLOP WITH ELDERFLOWER VINEGAR & GARLIC CAPERS /
GRILLED SCALLOP WITH GARLIC BUTTER

SERVES 4

8 large scallops, cleaned,
 in their shells
4 teaspoons elderflower vinegar
 (see page 262)
1 tablespoon lemon juice, plus
 extra for spritzing
2 tablespoons first-press
 rapeseed oil
12 garlic capers (see page 271)
salt and freshly ground
 black pepper

FOR THE GARLIC BUTTER

2 bunches of flat-leaf parsley,
 stalks discarded
2 roasted garlic bulbs (see page
 267), flesh squeezed out
1 garlic clove
1 tablespoon rapeseed oil
1 good pinch of salt
250g unsalted butter, at
 room temperature

First, make the garlic butter. Put a large saucepan of salted water on to boil. Have a bowl of iced water ready to the side. Blanch the parsley in the boiling water for 3 minutes, then scoop it out with a slotted spoon and place it immediately into the iced water. Drain and transfer it to a food processor, along with the roasted garlic, garlic clove, rapeseed oil and salt and blend to a smooth paste. Fold this into the soft butter and then mix until incorporated. Transfer to an airtight container and refrigerate until needed.

Using a spoon, remove 4 of the scallops from their shells and cut each one into 4 pieces. Place the pieces in a small mixing bowl and add the elderflower vinegar, lemon juice and rapeseed oil. Season with salt, tasting to check the balance of flavours, adding more salt or lemon juice if needed, before adding the pieces of scallop back into the shells. Top each with 3 garlic capers. Set aside.

Preheat the grill to high. Season the 4 remaining scallops with salt and pepper in their shells. Place them in a lined grill pan and dot each with a small tablespoon of the garlic butter. Grill for 2–3 minutes, depending on size, until cooked through. (Alternatively, you can cook them in the oven at 220°C/200°C fan/Gas Mark 7 for 2–3 minutes.) Finish each scallop with a spritz of lemon juice and serve alongside the cold scallops straight away.

Creating delicious sauces from humble ingredients and trimmings is one of the reasons that I love cooking so much. Though the ingredients list is long in this recipe the method is straightforward and the result decadent and rich.

Grilled red mullet
WITH A SAUCE MADE FROM THE BONES

SERVES 4

4 bones and heads of red
  mullet, washed
4 vine tomatoes, off the vine
2 tablespoons cooking oil, plus
  extra to oil the fish
1 fennel bulb, sliced
1 onion, sliced
1 carrot, peeled and sliced
3 celery sticks, destringed and
  cut into 1cm pieces
1 garlic clove, crushed
1 bay leaf
1 star anise
1 teaspoon coriander seeds
5 black peppercorns
1 pinch of paprika
1 tablespoon tomato purée
1 unwaxed orange, zested, then
  peeled and sliced
150ml white wine
25ml white vermouth
100g unsalted butter
1 teaspoon lemon juice
8 red mullet fillets
  (about 100g each)
salt and freshly ground
  black pepper

Preheat the oven to 200°C/180°C fan/Gas Mark 6.

Place the mullet bones and heads in a baking tray with the tomatoes. Roast for 15 minutes, until the fish bones are golden brown and the tomatoes are roasted. Add about 100ml of water to the baking tray. Using a wooden spoon, give the bottom a good scrape until you've released all the flavourful stuck-on bits. Set aside.

Heat the oil in a large saucepan over a medium–high heat. When hot, add the fennel, onion, carrot, celery, garlic, bay leaf, star anise, coriander seeds and peppercorns and cook for 6–8 minutes, until you get a nice amount of colour on the vegetables. Season with a good amount of salt, and add the paprika and the tomato purée. Cook for a further 1 minute, stirring well, then the orange zest and flesh and the roasted fish bones.

Cook for a further 5 minutes, then add the wine and vermouth. Bring to a simmer and allow to reduce a little for about 1 minute, then add the liquid from the tray of bones and 1 litre of water. Reduce the heat and simmer for about 30 minutes, then strain all the liquid into a fresh pan (take care not to waste any).

Add the roasted tomatoes to the liquid in the fresh pan, then the butter. Place over a high heat and reduce for about 10 minutes, until about one-third of the liquid has evaporated. Remove from the heat and, using a stick blender, blitz well. Check the seasoning and add the lemon juice to finish. Set aside while you cook the fish.

Preheat the grill to high. Brush each fillet on both sides with cooking oil. Season both sides of the fillets with salt and pepper and on a lined baking tray. Grill the fish for 2–3 minutes, depending on their size, until just cooked (pick up the fish to check, if you like). Place the fillets on serving plates with puddles of the warm sauce.

Whilst shop bought pickled herring can be pretty good, pickled at home they are taken to quite another level. When pickling fish you need the freshest available and, as herring seem to decide their own seasons to appear, snap them up when you can. Ask your fishmonger to butterfly them for you. Once made they will keep for up to two weeks in the fridge.

You will need to start this dish at least two days in advance of when you want to serve.

Cider pickled herrings
SERVED WITH RADICCHIO & APPLE

SERVES 4

sea salt, for curing, plus
    extra to season
6 herring, butterflied
300ml cider vinegar
100g caster sugar
1 teaspoon mustard seeds
1 teaspoon peppercorns
3 bay leaves
100ml cider

FOR THE SALAD
1 red onion, thinly sliced
1 head of radicchio,
    leaves separated
1 eating apple (such as Granny
    Smith), cored and sliced
1 tablespoon rapeseed oil

Sprinkle some sea salt over a baking tray and place the butterflied herring, skin-sides downwards, on top. Season the flesh sides well with salt. Cover the herrings and refrigerate overnight to cure.

Put the cider vinegar, sugar, mustard seeds, peppercorns, bay leaves and 75ml of water in a small saucepan over a medium heat. Bring to the boil, then add the cider. Remove from the heat and set aside to cool completely – this is your pickling liquid. Remove the fish from the fridge. Sprinkle the sliced onion over and pour over all the pickling liquid so that the fillets are submerged. Return to the fridge and leave for 24 hours before serving.

Make the salad. Place the red onion and radicchio leaves in a bowl along with the apple. Sprinkle over the rapeseed oil, season with salt and combine.

Drain the herrings from their pickling liquid and serve alongside the salad.

Steamed fish is very under rated these days but for me it's one of the purest ways of cooking fish. The texture you get, especially with a beautiful piece of turbot, is just amazing and only needs a delicious dressing to accompany. The inspiration for this dish came from one of our regulars at Root who told us of the days long past when he would be served fish with a tin of tangerines and some stem ginger – 'horrible' he said, but I thought there was something in that combination and so put this dish on the menu. It is anything but horrible!

Don't forget that you can keep the tops, tails and outer leaves of the leeks to make things like leek oil (see page 268) or leek powder (see page 271), or use them when you make stock.

Steamed turbot
WITH LEEKS, STEM GINGER & BLOOD ORANGE DRESSING

SERVES 4

FOR THE TURBOT
1 tablespoon sea salt
1 teaspoon caster sugar
4 skin-on boneless turbot fillets
   (about 120g each)

FOR THE LEEKS
1 leek, outer layer peeled, then
   topped, tailed and cut into
   2cm slices
2 tablespoons first-press rapeseed
   oil, plus extra to finish the fish
1 tablespoon lemon juice, plus
   extra to finish the fish
leek oil (see page 268), to finish
leek powder (see page 271),
   to finish
salt and freshly ground
   black pepper

FOR THE BLOOD ORANGE DRESSING
1 blood orange, segmented
100g drained stem ginger, chopped
   into fine dice
1 tablespoon stem ginger syrup
   from the jar
2 tablespoons rapeseed oil
salt

Make a cure by combining the sea salt and sugar and scatter evenly over the flesh of the fish. Place the fillets skin-sides downwards in a large tray (large enough to hold the turbot). Refrigerate for at least 30 minutes.

While the fish is curing, make the leeks and dressing. Place the prepared leeks in a lined baking tray, dress with the oil and lemon juice and season with salt and pepper. Set aside.

For the dressing, first, in a bowl, cut the orange segments into 4 or 5 pieces each – you need the bowl so that you can collecting the juice as you go. Tip the diced stem ginger into the bowl along with the syrup, orange segments and juice and rapeseed oil. Season with a little salt and stir gently to combine.

Place the cured fish, skin sides upwards, and the leeks on the same tier in a steamer (or in the steaming tray of a saucepan). Steam for 5 minutes, until the fish is cooked so that the skin peels away easily, leaving you with 4 perfect skinless fish fillets, and the leeks are tender.

To serve, place 4 or 5 pieces of leek on each plate. Top each serving of leeks with a fish fillet and spoon the dressing over. Finish with a little leek oil and powder and a splash of lemon juice and sprinkling of salt.

Mussels with curry sauce is an unexpected flavour match but an absolute winner. Adjust the spice if you wish – I'm not great with heat so the balance for my taste is perfect but by all means ramp it up if you want more of a hit.

You can make the curry sauce in advance and keep it in an airtight container in the fridge for up to five days. Or, it will freeze well if you want to store it for longer before using.

Mussels cooked in a light almond curry sauce
& FRESH CORIANDER

SERVES 4

3 tablespoons cooking oil
2 shallots, sliced
1kg mussels, cleaned
200ml white wine
1 bunch of coriander, chopped
1 tablespoon lemon juice
salt and freshly ground
    black pepper

FOR THE CURRY SAUCE
3 tablespoons cooking oil
2 shallots, sliced
1 roasted garlic bulb (see page
    267), flesh squeezed out
1 red chilli, deseeded and sliced
6cm piece of fresh root ginger,
    peeled and sliced
1 carrot, peeled and sliced
2 tablespoons mild curry powder
1 tablespoon ground turmeric
1 good pinch of salt
1 banana, sliced
2 apples, peeled, cored and sliced
100g whole blanched almonds
125ml white wine

First, make the curry sauce. Heat the oil in a heavy-based saucepan over a medium heat. When hot, add the shallots, garlic, chilli, ginger and carrot. Cook for 2–3 minutes, stirring well, then add the curry powder, turmeric and good pinch of salt. Sweat the vegetables for a further 5 minutes, until you start to get some colour on them (this is a good thing). Add the banana, apples and almonds and cook for 2–3 minutes, until the apple has softened. Add the wine, stirring well to get any flavour off the bottom of the pan, then bring to a simmer and cook for 1 minute, until the liquid has reduced by half. Add 2 litres of water, turn down the heat to a low simmer and cook for 20 minutes, until the ingredients are soft. Remove from the heat and allow to cool slightly. Then, using a hand-held stick blender, blitz until smooth. Set aside and keep warm.

To cook the mussels, heat the oil in a large saucepan over a medium heat. When hot, add the shallots and cook for 2 minutes, until softened, then add the mussels and turn up the heat. Add the white wine and a couple of large ladlefuls of curry sauce. (Keep the remaining curry sauce for another meal such as the celeriac curry on page 98.) Place a lid on the pan and cook for 2–3 minutes, then remove the lid. All the mussels should have opened (discard any that haven't). Taste the sauce for seasoning (adding salt if needed), then stir through the coriander and the lemon juice and serve immediately.

I love the intense flavour of smoked haddock and for me poaching is the way to make the most of this amazing fish. This wonderful dish first came about when we discovered that the leftover creamy liquid in which we poached our haddock had the most incredible flavour, almost tastier than the fish itself. So we decided to use it all – the fish and the poaching liquid – to make these fantastic arancini. Use un-dyed smoked haddock fillets and cook in one piece for best results.

Smoked haddock arancini

MAKES 24 OR 12 LARGER

1 large smoked haddock fillet
   (about 800g)
600ml whole milk
200ml double cream
1 pinch of paprika
1 pinch of turmeric
1 pinch of mild curry powder
1 bay leaf
4 peppercorns
1 teaspoon fennel seeds
1 garlic clove, crushed

FOR THE ARANCINI
2 tablespoons cooking oil, plus
   extra for deep-frying
2 shallots, diced
1 roasted garlic bulb (see page
   267), flesh squeezed out
1 garlic clove, minced
1 pinch of salt, plus extra to season
1 teaspoon smoked paprika
200g risotto rice
200ml white wine
120g Cheddar cheese, grated
50g unsalted butter
1 tablespoon sherry vinegar
juice of 1 lemon
1 teaspoon Tabasco sauce
100g plain flour
3 eggs, beaten
250g dried breadcrumbs
   (use panko, if possible)

Place all the ingredients, except those for the arancini, into a large saucepan with 200ml of water, ensuring the fish is submerged (top up with extra water if necessary). Place over a low heat, slowly bring to the boil, then remove from the heat and cover the pan, letting the fish poach in the residual heat for about 10–15 minutes, until cooked and the flesh flakes nicely away from the skin. Drain, reserving the poaching liquid, discard the skin and flake the flesh. Set aside until needed.

To make the arancini, heat the 2 tablespoons of oil in a large saucepan over a medium heat. When hot, add the shallots, both garlics, and the salt and paprika and sweat for 2 minutes, stirring well, until softened. Add the risotto rice and stir to coat the rice, adding a little oil if the pan looks dry. Cook the rice for a further 1 minute, then add the wine and stir to deglaze the pan. Cook for 1 minute, until the liquid has gone, and add the first ladle of the reserved poaching liquid, stirring well to ensure the mixture isn't sticking to the bottom of the pan.

Keep adding the poaching liquid one ladleful at a time, stirring continuously and allowing each ladleful to be absorbed before adding the next, until you have used all the liquid. The whole process should take about 20 minutes, at which point you will have rice that is tender but still with a little bite. Add the Cheddar, butter, vinegar, lemon juice and Tabasco and cook for a further 2 minutes, stirring, until the rice is completely tender and the butter and cheese have melted.

Remove the pan from the heat and fold through the flaked fish. Check the seasoning, then spread out the mixture on a baking tray and leave to cool. Once cool, cover and refrigerate for 1 hour, until set firm.

Remove the hardened rice mixture from the fridge. Take small portions of the mixture (about 50g each; or make 12 larger balls of 100g each) and roll between your palms into 24 arancini balls. Place the balls into a lined baking tray and return them to the fridge for a further 5 minutes to firm up again.

...method continued on page 196

Place the flour in one bowl, the beaten egg in a second bowl and the breadcrumbs in a third. Making sure each ball is fully coated at each stage, one by one, dip the arancini into the flour, then into the beaten egg and finally into the breadcrumbs, gently shaking off any excess.

Pour the cooking oil into a deep pan until two-thirds full and heat the oil to 180°C on a cooking thermometer or until a cube of day-old bread turns golden in 60 seconds (or preheat a deep-fat fryer to 180°C). A few at a time, place the arancini balls into the oil and cook for 2–3 minutes, turning with a slotted spoon, until golden all over. Set aside each batch to drain on kitchen paper, while you fry the next (you can keep them warm in a low oven, if you like). (If you have made larger arancini place them in a 200°C/180°C fan/Gas Mark 6 oven to warm through.) Serve straight away.

Pork belly is a wonderful and very versatile cut that never disappoints. This simple, delicious recipe can be prepared well in advance and is really no more than slicing and frying. No crackling here but the meat is wonderfully tender and the frying gives a delicious crust. Ask your butcher for the skin and you can cook it separately and serve alongside or enjoy it as a snack.

If you want to get ahead with your meal, you can cook the pork belly, roll it in cling film and leave it in the fridge for three to five days before cooking.

Rolled & braised pork belly
WITH BURNT APPLE PURÉE, CELERY & FRESH APPLE

SERVES 6

1.5–2kg skinned and boned pork
    belly (prepared weight)
brine (see page 258), to cover
    the meat
1 tablespoon Dijon mustard
1 tablespoon Worcestershire
    sauce
1 tablespoon first-press rapeseed
    oil, plus extra for frying
3 teaspoons paprika
1 teaspoon light brown soft sugar
1 teaspoon chilli powder
1 teaspoon garlic powder
1 teaspoon onion powder

FOR THE BURNT APPLE PURÉE
4 cooking apples, peeled,
    quartered and cored
100g caster sugar
1 pinch of sea salt

TO SERVE
1 celery stick, destringed and sliced
1 Granny Smith apple,
    cored and sliced

Preheat the oven to 180°C/160°C fan/Gas Mark 4.

Place the pork belly in a large baking tray or other vessel in which it can sit flat. Pour in enough brine to submerge the meat and refrigerate for 2 hours. This helps season the meat dramatically, making it juicier and tastier. After brining, rinse the pork to remove the brine residue.

Put the mustard, Worcestershire sauce, rapeseed oil, paprika, sugar and chilli, garlic and onion powders in a small mixing bowl and whisk well. When the brining is done, using your hands spread the spice mixture all over the meat. Take hold of one long side of the pork belly and roll it up to create a long sausage shape. Using butcher's string, tie the roll in place.

Pour a small amount of water into a baking tray (you need about 3cm depth), place the pork belly roll on top and cover first with a piece of baking paper and then with a piece of foil. Roast in the oven for 2½–3 hours, depending on the size of the pork belly, until the meat easily yields to a sharp knife.

While the pork belly is roasting, make the apple purée. Place the apple pieces and sugar in a bowl, turning the apple to coat fully. Place a large saucepan on a high heat. Add the sugary apples and cook for about 5 minutes, turning often, to really burn the sugar around the apples – to the point where they look like it's all gone wrong and the apples are fully caught and caramelised. Add 200ml of water, bring to the boil and allow to cook, scraping the bottom of the pan to get all the burnt bits, for 2 minutes, until the apples are soft and the water has reduced to almost nothing.

Transfer the apple mixture to a food processor and blitz the purée until it's silky smooth, adding a little water to help achieve the right consistency, if necessary. Taste and finish with the pinch of sea salt. Cool and transfer to an airtight container. Refrigerate until the pork is ready.

...method continued on page 198

When cooked, you can slice and serve the pork straight away with the apple purée. However, to get a perfect cylinder and crust on the pork takes a little more time and a bit of preparation.

Remove the pork from the oven and leave, covered, until cool enough to handle.

Lay out a sheet of cling film on your work surface. Transfer the pork belly to the cling film and wrap it tightly to create a cylinder shape. Place in the fridge to cool and set for 56 hours, or overnight.

To serve, unwrap the pork belly from the cling film and snip off and discard the string. Slice the belly into 2–3cm-thick rounds. Heat up a little oil in a frying pan over a medium heat. Place the pork belly rounds about 3 at a time (depending on the size of your pork belly and pan) into the pan and cook for 5–6 minutes on each side, until caramelised and hot throughout (take care – the fat will spit).

Divide the pork equally among 4 plates. Top with spoonfuls of the apple purée, and the sliced celery and sliced apple to serve.

It wasn't until I worked at Josh Eggleton's Michelin star pub The Pony & Trap in Chew Magna that I began to cook with every part of the animal and the joys of offal and the head to toe philosophy became my norm. Whilst it's still a joy to cook a big fat steak there is now something even more enjoyable about serving up a dish like this brilliant dripping toast with ox tongue sauce – a dish of which my dad and grandparents would be proud!

The tongue will keep well in the fridge for three to five days. You can use it in many different ways, such as sliced thinly in a sandwich or in a salad.

Fried duck egg on beef dripping toast
WITH OX TONGUE SAUCE

SERVES 4

1 brined ox tongue
200ml red wine
2 thyme sprigs
2 bay leaves
5 peppercorns
1 shallot, chopped
2 garlic cloves, crushed
500g reduced beef stock
4 tablespoons cooking oil
4 duck eggs, to serve
salt and freshly ground
    black pepper

FOR THE TOAST
100g aged beef fat or dripping
4 slices of good bread

Preheat the oven to 180°C/160°C fan/Gas Mark 4.

Place the ox tongue into a casserole or oven-safe pan along with the wine, thyme, bay leaves, peppercorns, shallot and garlic, and add enough water to cover. Place over a high heat and bring up to a simmer, then place in the oven for 3–4 hours, checking regularly, and topping up with water if necessary, until you can pierce it with a small knife but it still retains some resistance. Remove from the oven and leave the tongue in the liquid until cool enough to handle.

Remove and discard the tough outer skin from the tongue and refrigerate the tongue to cool completely and firm up (about 30 minutes). Once the tongue has cooled, dice it into 1cm pieces and set aside.

While the tongue is cooling, pour the beef stock into a saucepan and place over a medium heat. Bring to the simmer and allow to reduce for about 5–10 minutes, until you have a nice gravy consistency. Add the diced tongue and keep warm while you fry the eggs and make the toast.

Heat the oil in a frying pan on a low heat and crack in the eggs. Fry for about 3–5 minutes, until the whites are firm and the yolks are still runny. Season well with salt and pepper.

While the eggs are frying, make the toasts. Heat a griddle or frying pan to medium hot. Spread the fat or dripping on to the bread, then grill or fry for 90 seconds each side, until crispy and toasted.

Place a slice of toast on each plate. Top with a fried egg and good lashings of gravy and tongue.

Steak tartare is one of my all-time favourite dishes –
if it's on the menu then I'm having it. The Onglet cut,
also known as hanger steak, has an amazing flavour
and texture.

Onglet tartare
WITH RAW EGG YOLK & MATCHSTICK FRIES

SERVES 4

2 large Maris Piper potatoes
600g trimmed onglet steak
4 tablespoons capers, chopped
4 tablespoons cornichons,
    chopped
2 banana shallots, diced
4 tablespoons chopped parsley
4 dashes of Tabasco sauce
2 tablespoons tomato ketchup
2 tablespoons Worcestershire
    sauce
1 teaspoon English mustard
1 teaspoon lemon juice
1 teaspoon sherry vinegar
1 tablespoon first-press
    rapeseed oil
2 good pinches of freshly ground
    black pepper
cooking oil, for frying
4 individual egg yolks (optional),
    to serve
sea salt

First make the matchstick fries. Using the smaller blade attachment on a
mandolin, carefully shred the potatoes into 'matchstick' pieces. Place the
matchsticks in a bowl and wash them under running water until the water
runs clear (indicating that the starches have washed off). Leave the fries in
water until you're ready to cook.

Trim the onglet of all the sinew and dice into roughly 1cm pieces. Place the
pieces in a mixing bowl and add all the remaining ingredients except the
cooking oil and egg yolks. Season with a good amount of salt and mix well
with a spoon. Check the seasoning and adjust the flavours, adding more
Tabasco, ketchup, mustard, salt or pepper and so on, if necessary. Set aside
while you make the fries (you don't want the meat too cold when you serve,
as it will detract from the flavours).

Pour the cooking oil into a deep saucepan until two-thirds full and heat the
oil to 180°C on a cooking thermometer or until a cube of day-old bread
turns golden in 60 seconds (or preheat a deep-fat fryer to 180°C). Dry the
fries a little on kitchen paper, then drop them into the oil and cook for about
2 minutes, until crispy and golden brown. Scoop out the fries and drain well
on kitchen paper, then season with sea salt.

To serve, place equal amounts of the steak tartare on each plate and, if
serving with an egg yolk, make a little well in the centre. Pop an egg yolk into
each well and serve with fries on the side.

This chicken schnitzel has its origins in a recipe made one day by Jordan Meagher for a staff lunch at Root. It was just fantastic and was put straight onto the menu where it has stayed ever since. The brining process produces a wonderful depth of flavour and the anchovies are a joyous addition to the fried chicken.

Chicken schnitzel
WITH GARLIC, PARMESAN & FRESH ANCHOVIES

SERVES 4

4 skinless, boneless chicken thighs
100g plain flour
2 eggs, beaten
150g dried breadcrumbs
    (use panko, if possible)
cooking oil, for frying
100g garlic butter
    (see page 268), softened
150g Parmesan, grated
12 fresh anchovy fillets
sea salt

FOR THE BRINE
60g salt
40g caster sugar
1 bay leaf
5 peppercorns
2 thyme sprigs
pared peel of 1 lemon

Make the brine. Put all the ingredients into a large saucepan with 600ml of water and give it all a good whisk. Place over a high heat and heat for 5 minutes, until the sugar and salt have dissolved. Allow to cool completely.

Place the chicken thighs in a large bowl. Pour over the brine (make sure the meat is fully submerged), cover and refrigerate for 45 minutes, then drain, rinse and pat dry.

Preheat the oven to 200°C/180°C fan/Gas Mark 6.

When the chicken is ready, place the flour in one bowl, the beaten egg in a second bowl and the breadcrumbs in a third. Making sure the chicken is well coated at each stage, one by one dip the thighs into the flour, then into the beaten egg and finally into the breadcrumbs, gently shaking off any excess.

Pour the cooking oil into a deep pan until two-thirds full and heat the oil to 180°C on a cooking thermometer or until a cube of day-old bread turns golden in 60 seconds (or preheat a deep-fat fryer to 180°C). Add the chicken thighs and cook for 4–5 minutes, turning regularly, until cooked through, golden brown and crisp all over. Remove the chicken from the oil, drain on kitchen paper and season with sea salt.

Transfer the fried chicken to a baking tray, cover with the softened garlic butter and sprinkle over the Parmesan. Bake for 3–5 minutes, until the butter has melted and the Parmesan is golden. Remove from the oven and leave to rest for 1 minute before slicing and serving with the anchovies across the top.

I have Josh Eggleton to thank for this fantastic recipe – it is a Pony & Trap classic and has been on their Michelin star menu for ever and a day. Sweetbreads, the glands from the throat, heart or stomach of a calf or lamb, are delicate in flavour, creamy in texture and when combined with the marmite and the maple truly amazing.

You can prepare the sweetbreads in advance: cook and peel them, then keep them in the fridge for up to two to three days.

Marmite & maple-glazed lamb sweetbreads

SERVES 4

1 onion, chopped
1 carrot, peeled and chopped
2 garlic cloves, crushed
1 leek top, chopped
1 bay leaf
1 thyme sprig
1 teaspoon fennel seeds
1 teaspoon black peppercorns
1 tablespoon white wine vinegar
100ml white wine
10g salt
300g sweetbreads
1 tablespoon plain flour
2 tablespoons cooking oil
salt and freshly ground
   black pepper

FOR THE GLAZE
1 tablespoon Marmite
1 tablespoon maple syrup
250ml shop-bought, fresh beef
   stock, reduced to 100ml and
   kept warm (or make up with a
   stock cube)

Rinse the sweetbreads under cold running water. Set aside.

Place all the other ingredients except the flour and cooking oil all in a large saucepan. Place over a medium heat and add 1 litre of water. Bring to the boil, then reduce the heat to give you a good simmer. Add the sweetbreads and cook for 6–8 minutes, until firmed up and holding their shape. Using a slotted spoon, remove the sweetbreads from the stock and set aside on a baking tray until cool enough to handle. Peel off the membrane and the sinew from around the sweetbreads.

In a mixing bowl, pull apart the sweetbreads so they are roughly the same size. Tip the flour into a bowl and season well with salt and black pepper. Add the sweetbreads to the flour and toss to coat.

In a separate bowl, combine the glaze ingredients and set aside.

Heat the oil in a frying pan over a medium heat. When hot, add the flour-dusted sweetbreads to the pan. Cook on both sides for about 3–4 minutes, until they have a good, golden crust all over. Add the glaze and cook again for 1 minute, turning regularly, until beautifully glazed all over. Serve and enjoy straight away.

It is a truth not well known that most ox heart is sold off by local butchers for dog food. Lovely for the dog population but a terrible waste for us humans. This recipe reclaims the ox heart for the kitchen. There is a bit of wastage when preparing the heart but with time and practice you can end up with the most amazing pieces of meat which, when flash fried, are right up there with the very best cuts of beef.

Grilled ox heart
WITH PICKLED RED CABBAGE & WATERCRESS

SERVES 4

400g ox-heart meat (ask your
    butcher to prepare it for you)
2 tablespoons cooking oil
garlic clove, crushed
20g unsalted butter
200g watercress
salad dressing (see page 259)
salt and freshly ground
    black pepper

FOR THE PICKLED RED CABBAGE
1 red cabbage, outer leaves
    discarded, quartered, cored
    and thinly shredded
10g sea salt
2 bay leaves
1 teaspoon coriander seeds
pickle liquid (see page 258)

Start with the pickled cabbage. Place the shredded cabbage in a mixing bowl. Add the salt and mix well, working it into the cabbage to help break it down, then add the bay leaves and coriander seeds. Transfer the mixture to an airtight container, cover with pickle liquid and seal with the lid for about 12 hours if possible. (This will make more than you need for the dish, but keep any leftovers in the fridge for up to a week, using it in other salads, as you like.)

Heat a griddle pan or frying pan until hot. Rub the ox-heart meat with the oil and season with salt and pepper, then add it to the hot pan. Cook on both sides, for 2 minutes each. Add the crushed garlic clove and the butter, allowing the butter to melt until foaming and golden. Use the melted butter to baste the heart for about 1 minute, then remove from the heat and rest well for about 3–5 minutes. Thinly slice the heart against the grain – the meat should be cooked to medium, a little pink in the centre.

In a mixing bowl toss the watercress with the dressing and season with a little salt. Drain the pickled cabbage (discard the pickling liquid) and add it to the watercress. Arrange it on a serving platter and top with the sliced meat. When you serve, make sure each person gets a good amount of meat.

Brining a chicken ahead of frying gives it that extra bit of oomph and when matched with my gooseberry jam and sauerkraut then all the right flavour notes are hit. Fantastic!

You will need to prepare the sauerkraut at least five days in advance of when you want to serve, and you'll need to make the gooseberry jam in advance, too.

Buttermilk fried chicken
WITH SAUERKRAUT & GOOSEBERRY JAM

SERVES 4

4 boneless, skin-on chicken
  thighs (each about 120g)
1 litre cooking oil
500g buttermilk
dredge (see page 263)

FOR THE SAUERKRAUT
1 white cabbage, halved,
  cored and shredded
2 per cent of the weight of the
  shredded cabbage in sea salt

FOR THE GOOSEBERRY JAM
1kg gooseberries, topped
  and tailed (or use
  ready-prepped frozen)
150ml white wine
100ml white wine vinegar
250g caster sugar
5g sea salt

FOR THE BRINE
60g salt
40g caster sugar
1 bay leaf
5 peppercorns
2 thyme sprigs
pared peel of 1 lemon

To make the sauerkraut, massage the sea salt into the cabbage until it releases enough liquid to cover. This will take about 10 minutes, if you work at it hard! Store in an airtight container at room temperature for 5–7 days, until fermented.

For the gooseberry jam, place all the ingredients into a large saucepan over a medium–low heat. Bring to a simmer and cook for 15 minutes, stirring regularly, until the mixture is thick and jammy (remember that once it's cool it will thicken up a bit more, so judge accordingly). Remove from the heat and leave to cool.

Make the brine. Put all the ingredients into a large saucepan with 600ml of water and give it all a good whisk. Place over a high heat and heat for 5 minutes, until the sugar and salt have dissolved. Allow to cool completely.

Pour the brine into a large bowl or pan. Add the chicken so that it is completely submerged and refrigerate for 45 minutes. Remove the chicken thighs and give them a slight rinse in running water.

Pour the cooking oil into a deep pan until two-thirds full and heat the oil to 180°C on a cooking thermometer or until a cube of day-old bread turns golden in 60 seconds (or preheat a deep-fat fryer to 180°C).

Pour the buttermilk into one mixing bowl and tip the dredge into another. One by one, dip the chicken thighs into buttermilk and then into the dredge, making sure each thigh is well coated.

In batches, cook the thighs in the oil for about 4–5 minutes, turning, until the chicken is cooked through and golden and crispy on the outside. Remove the thighs from the oil using a slotted spoon and set aside to drain well on kitchen paper. Serve warm alongside the sauerkraut and the jam.

I consider this dish to be an essential for any meat lover's repertoire. Serve the ragú with anything and everything – meat, fish, pasta, salads, vegetables, sandwiches, it all works. This ragú keeps well in the fridge for up to five days, or freeze it for up six months.

Ox cheek ragú

SERVES 4

4 trimmed ox cheeks
   (about 1kg altogether)
3 tablespoons cooking oil
1 onion, chopped
1 carrot, peeled and chopped
1 leek, chopped
3 celery sticks, chopped
3 garlic cloves, crushed
2 bay leaves
4 thyme sprigs
1 teaspoon black peppercorns
500ml red wine
2 bunches of red grapes, picked ·
1 tablespoon Dijon mustard
1 tablespoon balsamic vinegar
salt and freshly ground
   black pepper

Preheat the oven to 200°C /180°C fan/Gas Mark 6.

Season the ox cheeks with salt and pepper. Heat the cooking oil in an ovenproof pan or casserole dish over a medium heat. Add the ox cheeks and cook for about 5 minutes on each side, until well coloured (do this in batches, if necessary). Remove the browned cheeks from the pan and set aside on a plate to rest. Add the vegetables, bay, thyme and peppercorns to the pan, cook for a couple of minutes until the vegetables are a little coloured, then add the red wine and grapes. Return the ox cheeks to the pan and add water to cover. Put the lid on the pan or cover the pan with foil and transfer to the oven. Cook for about 3½ hours, or until the ox cheek is tender and falling apart.

Remove the cheeks from the liquid and transfer to a bowl. Using your hands, gently pull the meat apart slightly, not fully shredding it, as it will break down further when you mix it back through the sauce. Pick out any gristle or tough bits in the meat and discard.

Pour the cooking liquid through a sieve into a clean saucepan (really pushing all the liquid though the sieve to make sure you get all the flavour especially out of the grapes). Discard the contents of the sieve. Place the pan with the sauce over a high heat and bring to a simmer. Cook for 10–15 minutes, until the liquid has reduced to become thick and rich.

Add the meat to the saucepan and mix gently so that the sauce coats the meat. Keep the ragú on the heat and reduce it further, if necessary. Stir through the Djion mustard and balsamic vinegar and check the seasoning. Serve however you wish.

desserts

These doughnut delights are an absolute favourite on our menu! Though I am not a massive evangelist for the use of vegetables in desserts, this just works. Carrots have long shown themselves irresistible in Britain's favourite cake, which was the inspiration for this jam and where they work just as well and are equally as delicious.

Carrot jam-filled doughnuts
WITH MASCARPONE VANILLA CREAM

MAKES ABOUT 15

220ml whole milk
500g strong white bread flour
15g fresh yeast
60g caster sugar
100g unsalted butter, softened
10g salt
2 eggs
1 egg yolk
cooking oil, for frying

FOR THE CARROT JAM
300g carrots, peeled and sliced
200ml carrot juice
180g caster sugar

FOR THE MASCARPONE CREAM
200g mascarpone
1 teaspoon vanilla seeds (scraped from about ½ vanilla pod)
2 tablespoons icing sugar, sifted
50ml double cream

Heat the milk in a small saucepan over a very low heat, until just lukewarm (you just want to take the edge off it). Remove from the heat and set aside. Add the flour, yeast and sugar to the bowl of a stand mixer fitted with the dough hook. Turn on the mixer on low speed and mix in the softened butter and salt until everything is well combined. Add the eggs and egg yolk, then, once fully incorporated, add the lukewarm milk. Turn up the speed of the mixer to medium–high and beat for 6–8 minutes, until the dough is coming away from the sides of the bowl and is looking glossy. It is a rich dough, so can be sticky, but with enough time it will be easy to handle.

Tip out the dough on to a clean work surface. Use your hands to bring the dough together to form a nice, smooth ball, then place it back into the bowl and cover with a damp cloth. Leave it to rise in a warm place for about 30 minutes, or until at least doubled in size.

While the dough is rising, make the carrot jam. Place the ingredients with 300ml of water into a saucepan and place over a medium heat. Bring to the boil, then reduce the heat and simmer until there is little liquid left, the carrots are tender and the mixture looks jammy. Let the mixture cool slightly, then place in a food processor and blitz. Add a little extra water to the jam if it's too thick – you should be able to blend it nicely into a smooth purée. Transfer the jam to a clean container and set aside until needed. (If you don't use it all, keep the extra in sterilised jars and use it within 2 weeks.)

When the dough has risen, tip it out on to a clean work surface and divide it up into equal-sized balls of about 70g each (you should get about 15). Line a baking tray with baking paper and lightly dust it with flour. Roll the balls so that they are perfectly smooth (this can take a bit of practice, but persevere, as it gets easier). Place the balls on the tray, cover and leave to prove for about 20–30 minutes, until doubled in size.

...method continued on page 218

While the dough is proving, make the mascarpone cream. Put the mascarpone, vanilla and icing sugar in a mixing bowl and whisk well. In another bowl whisk the double cream to just under stiff peaks and fold this through the mascarpone mixture until fully combined. Set aside while you fry the doughnuts.

Pour the cooking oil into a deep pan until two-thirds full and heat to 180°C on a cooking thermometer or until a cube of day-old bread turns golden in 60 seconds (or preheat a deep-fat fryer to 180°C).

Once the doughnuts are ready to fry, carefully place 2 at a time into the oil, cooking for 5–6 minutes, turning every minute or so, so that they cook evenly and are golden all over. Using a slotted spoon, remove each batch from the oil and set aside on kitchen paper to drain while you repeat until you've cooked all the doughnuts.

When the doughnuts are cool enough to handle, use a skewer to pierce each one just to its centre (don't go all the way through), wiggling the skewer around to make a space for the jam in the middle, but without making the entrance hole too big. Transfer the jam into a piping bag fitted with a medium, round nozzle. Place the end of the piping nozzle into the holes and squeeze to fill the doughnuts with jam.

Tip the remaining sugar into a wide bowl. One by one, toss the doughnuts in the sugar, making sure they are well coated. Serve warm with the mascarpone cream on the side for dipping.

Pavlova, strawberries and cream – the quintessential British summertime dish. This is my take on that classic and, personally, I think it stands up very well in comparison. You can either make small individual meringues as here or just make one large one as a statement centre piece.

Pavlova
WITH 'STRAWBERRIES & CREAM'

SERVES 8

FOR THE STRAWBERRY JELLY
500g frozen strawberries
50g caster sugar, plus a little extra if using the carrageenan iota
4 mint sprigs, leaves picked, stalks reserved
3½ leaves of platinum-grade gelatine, soaked in water for 5 minutes, or 5g carrageenan iota

FOR THE MERINGUE
210g egg whites (about 7 eggs)
350g caster sugar

FOR THE CUSTARD
250ml double cream
1 teaspoon vanilla seeds (scraped from about 1 vanilla pod)
40g caster sugar
5 egg yolks

TO SERVE
1 large punnet of strawberries (about 500g), hulled and quartered

Make the strawberry jelly. Put the frozen strawberries, sugar and mint stalks in a heatproof bowl and cover with cling film. Place the bowl over a pan of simmering water (over a low heat) for about 20–30 minutes, to encourage the liquid to leach from the strawberries, then remove from the heat and leave the bowl, still covered, for a further 30 minutes on the side. Strain the liquid from the strawberries – you should have about 500ml. If you're short, top it up with water; if you have too much, increase the gelatine accordingly in the next step.

Place the liquid in a saucepan over a low heat and warm to just over 40°C on a sugar thermometer. Squeeze out the gelatine from its soaking water and add it to the pan. If you're using carrageenan iota, whisk it into a small amount of sugar, then whisk it into the liquid. Bring the liquid up to 80°C and simmer for 3 minutes, then pour through a sieve into a suitable container and refrigerate until set. It will need at least a few hours, but preferably overnight.

Preheat the oven to 120°C/100°C fan/Gas Mark ½–1.

For the meringue, using an electric whisk and a clean mixing bowl, slightly whisk the egg whites until frothy, then add the sugar 1 tablespoon at a time, whisking well between each addition. Once you've added all the sugar, continue whisking for about another 5 minutes, until you have glossy, stiff peaks that will hold if you turn the bowl upside down.

Place the meringue into a disposable pipping bag and cut 2.5cm from the end. On a silicone baking mat on a baking tray, pipe 8 meringue domes shapes, making sure you leave a good amount of space in between each dome. Using a warm spoon, make a divot in the top of each dome. Place the meringues in the oven and bake for 1 hour and 20 minutes, until the

...method continued on page 220

meringues are crispy on the outside and soft in the middle. Carefully remove from the oven and leave on the tray to cool. (If you're not using the meringues straight away place them in a sealed container and keep in a cool, dry place for up to 3 days.)

For the custard, bring the cream and vanilla to the boil in a saucepan over a medium heat. As soon as the mixture starts to boil, remove it from the heat. In a separate bowl, whisk together the sugar and egg yolks until pale and creamy. Pour a small amount of the hot cream mixture into the eggs-and-sugar mixture and whisk well. Little by little, add the cream to the eggs – do this slowly, taking care that the mixture doesn't curdle. Once fully combined, return the custard to the pan and put it back over a low heat. Stir for about 3 minutes, until the custard thickens so that it will coat the back of a spoon. If you want to go a little thicker, keep stirring over the heat until you reach your preferred consistency. Pour the custard into a warmed jug.

To serve, place one meringue in the centre of a plate and spoon jelly into the divot. Place a few cut strawberries over the top, then finish with a good sprig of mint (like any good dessert). Repeat for the remaining meringues, jelly, strawberries and mint. Serve with the jug of custard alongside.

Whilst growing up, a McFlurry was a top treat for me. This fantastic milk sorbet with its chocolate crumb takes me straight back to the drive thru ... it is delicious.

Milk sorbet
WITH A CHOCOLATE CRUMB

SERVES 6-8

FOR THE MILK SORBET
1 litre whole milk
1 tablespoon liquid glucose
6 tablespoons condensed milk
100g caster sugar

FOR THE CHOCOLATE CRUMB
200g caster sugar
135g 70% dark chocolate,
   broken into small pieces

For the sorbet, put 100ml of the milk in a bowl with the glucose and condensed milk and set aside. Place the rest of the milk in a large saucepan and add the sugar. Place over a medium heat and bring to a simmer. Allow to simmer, stirring well to stop the mixture catching, until reduced by half (about 5–10 minutes).

Pour into the bowl with the condensed milk mixture and whisk to make sure the glucose and condensed milk have melted. Leave to cool, then cover and place in the fridge to chill completely (about 1 hour). Once chilled, transfer the mixture to an ice-cream machine and churn until set. Scrape out the sorbet into a clean container and freeze for at least 2 hours before serving.

Make the chocolate crumb. Tip the sugar into a medium saucepan with 50ml of water. Place over a high heat and bring to the boil, then keep boiling until the temperature on a sugar thermometer reaches 130°C. Take the syrup off the heat and quickly add the chocolate, mixing well with a wooden spoon and scraping down the sides. Keep mixing, breaking up the contents of the pan until the mixture has cooled and you have a chocolate 'crumble'.

To serve, place scoops of the sorbet into a bowl and finish with a good sprinkling of chocolate crumb. Or, if you want the full flurry effect, allow the sorbet to soften in the fridge for 2–3 minutes, then scoop it into a piping bag fitted with a large star nozzle and pipe swirls into the bowls, then sprinkle with the crumb.

Lemon posset is a classic British dessert, and it's always welcome at a dinner party. The lemon curd is quite an effort so make a decent amount and use it for other dishes or simply enjoy with yoghurt. The chervil powder, though not essential, adds a lovely and unexpected herby note to this bold citrus-flavoured dish.

Lemon posset
WITH LEMON CURD, MERINGUE SHARDS & CHERVIL POWDER

SERVES 6

FOR THE LEMON POSSET
800g double cream
225g caster sugar
200ml lemon juice
   (about 4 or 5 lemons)
zest of 2 lemons
chervil powder (see page 271),
   optional, to serve

FOR THE LEMON CURD
225ml lemon juice
   (about 5 lemons)
zest of 3 lemons
100g unsalted butter
225g caster sugar
3 eggs and 3 eggs yolks,
   beaten together

FOR THE MERINGUE
110g egg whites
   (about 3 or 4 egg whites)
180g caster sugar

We use a tart ring wrapped in cling film for posset, but you could use a bowl.

To make the posset, put the cream in one saucepan and the caster sugar, lemon juice and lemon zest in another. Place both pans over a medium heat and bring to the boil. Reduce the heats and simmer for 30 seconds. then remove from the heat and pour the cream into the pan with the other ingredients. Whisk to combine and then let it sit for 2 minutes. Pour the mixture through a sieve into your mould, leave to cool, then transfer to the fridge for at least 6 hours, but ideally overnight, to set.

While the posset is setting, make the lemon curd (you'll have more than you need for this dessert, but you can store the remainder in a sterilised jar in the fridge – it's delicious on toast). Place a bowl over a pan of simmering water (don't let the base of the bowl touch the water) and add the lemon juice and zest, along with the butter and sugar. Whisk well until the butter has melted, then whisk in the beaten eggs. Keep whisking until the mixture has thickened and has taken on a custard-like texture – you'll need a good 10–15 minutes of whisking altogether. Remove the bowl from the heat and transfer to a clean bowl, cover the surface with cling film, then leave to cool and place in the fridge to thicken up for about 1 hour.

Make the meringue. Preheat the oven to 120°C/100°C fan/Gas Mark ½. Using an electric whisk and a clean mixing bowl, slightly whisk the egg whites until frothy, then add the sugar 1 tablespoon at a time. Once you've added all the sugar, continue whisking for about another 5 minutes, until you have glossy, stiff peaks that will hold if you turn the bowl upside down. Spread out the meringue in a thin layer over a silicone mat or a piece of baking paper. Slide on to a baking sheet and place in the oven. Cook the meringue for 1 hour, until dried and brittle, then remove from the oven and transfer (on the mat or baking paper) to a wire rack. (This will make more meringue than you need – store any leftovers for use another time.)

To serve, remove the posset from the fridge. If you've made it in a tart ring, place it on a plate and remove the ring. Spoon the lemon curd into a disposable piping bag, snip the end and dot a good amount of curd around the top of the posset. Break the meringue into shards and place over the posset and curd. Sprinkle the chervil powder, if using, over the top to finish.

Muller Rice was a regular treat growing up and I love them to this day – 'madeleine' memory flavours are always the best. This is Root's take on Muller Rice which we serve cold on top of an apple compote. The puddings can be made in advance and will keep very well in the fridge for a good few days along with the milk jam.

Rice pudding
WITH APPLE COMPOTE & MILK JAM

SERVES 4

FOR THE APPLE COMPOTE
20g caster sugar
3 large cooking apples, peeled, cored and thinly sliced
2 Granny Smith apples, peeled, cored and cut into 3mm dice

FOR THE MILK JAM
65g caster sugar
280ml whole milk
½ teaspoon bicarbonate of soda

FOR THE RICE PUDDING
100g pudding rice
650ml whole milk
50ml double cream
65g caster sugar
1 teaspoon vanilla seeds (scraped from ½ vanilla pod)
1 bay leaf
1 star anise
zest of 1 unwaxed lemon

First, make the apple compote. Tip the sugar into a medium saucepan and add the sliced cooking apples. Place the pan over a medium heat and allow the apples to break down for about 5 minutes, until soft. Transfer the apple mixture to a food processor and blitz until smooth. Return the purée to the pan and add the diced Granny Smiths. Place the pan over a low heat and cook the sauce for about 2–3 minutes, until the apples have softened. Remove from the heat and set aside.

Make the milk jam. Place all the ingredients into a small saucepan over a medium heat. Bring to the boil, then turn down the heat to a low simmer. Cook, whisking occasionally, for approximately 15–20 minutes until you have a dark brown caramel. Leave to cool. (Any leftovers will store in the fridge for up to 5 days.)

Rinse the pudding rice in a bowl and repeat until the water runs clear. Tip the rice into a large saucepan and add the remaining pudding ingredients. Place over a low heat and cook, stirring well, for 15 minutes, or until the rice is softened but still has a little bite.

Spoon the apple compote equally into the bottom of each bowl. Top with equal amounts of the rice pudding and spoonfuls of milk jam, adding as much as you wish. Serve warm or cold.

The brilliant Bristol Beer Factory brew their craft beer in the heart of Bristol. This combination of the stout sauce and the stout cake finished with the mint choc chip ice cream is like eating the most adult of kids' desserts imaginable. You can make the puddings in advance and reheat them in a microwave or steamer when you're ready to serve.

Bristol Beer Factory milk stout pudding
WITH STOUT SAUCE & MINT CHOCOLATE CHIP ICE CREAM

MAKES 8 PUDDINGS

FOR THE MINT CHOC CHIP ICE CREAM
1½ bunches of mint, leaves picked
120g 70% dark chocolate
ice-cream master base
 (see page 252)

FOR THE STOUT CAKE
250g unsalted butter,
 plus extra for greasing
250ml milk stout
85g cocoa powder
2 whole eggs
400g caster sugar
150g buttermilk
255g plain flour
3g baking powder
12g bicarbonate of soda
1 pinch of sea salt

FOR THE STOUT SAUCE
120ml milk stout
40g cocoa powder
100g caster sugar
1 teaspoon vanilla seeds (scraped
 from about ½ vanilla pod)
100g 70% dark chocolate,
 broken into small pieces

You'll need 15 x 175ml dariole
 moulds or mini pudding basins

First, make the ice cream. Place a saucepan of water on the heat and bring to a rapid boil. Have some iced water in a bowl ready on the side. Place the mint in the boiling water, making sure it is submerged. Cook for 2 minutes, until soft, then remove and immediately plunge it into the iced water to cool as quickly as possible. When cooled, drain the mint well. Put the chocolate into a food processor and pulse until broken up into small pieces that you can distribute through the ice cream.

Place the base ice cream into a blender and add the blanched mint. Blend until smooth and combined (you'll probably need to do this in 2 batches to get it as smooth as possible). Transfer the mixture to a suitable container and chill for 1 hour, until fully cold. Then, transfer to an ice-cream machine and churn until set. Transfer to a container and fold in the crushed chocolate. Freeze for at least 2 hours, then soften in the fridge for a few minutes before using, if necessary.

When you're ready to make the puddings, preheat the oven to 180°C/160°C fan/Gas Mark 4. Grease your moulds with a little bit of butter and place on a baking tray. Melt the butter in a saucepan over a medium heat with the stout and cocoa powder (about 5 minutes). In a large bowl, using a wooden spoon, beat together the eggs and sugar until light and fluffy. Add the melted butter mixture and the buttermilk and whisk to combine. Sift in the flour, baking powder, bicarbonate of soda and salt and whisk lightly to incorporate. Pour the batter equally into the moulds until it reaches two-thirds of the way up the sides and bake for 18–20 minutes, until a skewer inserted into each pudding comes out clean.

While the puddings are baking, make the sauce. Put the milk stout, cocoa powder, sugar and vanilla in a saucepan and place over a medium heat. Bring the mixture up to a simmer, whisking well, then cook for 60 seconds before adding the chocolate. Whisk again until the chocolate has melted and the mixture is fully combined. Set aside and keep warm.

Remove the cooked puddings from the oven, leave them to cool slightly in the moulds (so that they pop out easily), then turn out into individual serving bowls. Pour plenty of warm sauce into each bowl and top with a good ball of ice cream. Serve immediately.

Affogato, meaning 'drowned' in Italian, is a coffee-based dessert of ice cream or gelato with a slug of good hot espresso coffee poured over – I love it and it's a fantastic way to end a meal. The black sesame and orange tuille is our little twist on this classic and it marries amazingly well with the coffee. If you want to turn it up a little more then simply add a shot of liqueur such as Cointreau or amaretto.

The recipe will make more ice cream than you need for the affogato, but just keep it in the freezer for another time.

Black sesame affogato
WITH AN ORANGE SESAME TUILE

SERVES 6

150g black sesame seeds
ice-cream master base
   (see page 252)
6 shots of hot espresso coffee,
   to serve

FOR THE SESAME TUILE
100g plain flour
100g caster sugar
1 pinch of salt
30g black sesame seeds
30g white sesame seeds
100g unsalted butter, melted
100ml orange juice

Preheat the oven to 190°C/170°C fan/Gas Mark 5.

Place the black sesame seeds on to a baking tray and place in the oven to toast for 12–15 minutes. Remove from the oven and set aside to cool.

Put the ice-cream base into a blender and add the cooled, toasted sesame seeds. Blitz until as smooth as possible (it's best to do this in 2 batches). Pour the mixture into a suitable container and refrigerate for about 1 hour, until fully cold. Pour the mixture into your ice-cream machine and churn until set. Scrape into a container and freeze for at least 2 hours, then soften in the fridge for a few minutes before using, if necessary.

For the tuile, put the flour, sugar, salt and both sesame seeds in a mixing bowl. Add the melted butter along with the orange juice and whisk into a paste. Cover the bowl and refrigerate for 30 minutes. Spread the cooled mixture over a silicone mat (about 2mm thick), then place the mat on a baking tray. (You can use a special tuile mould for this, if you prefer.) Bake for 12–15 minutes, until evenly coloured. Remove from the oven and allow to cool for 5 minutes, then transfer to a cooling rack and leave to cool completely – the mixture will harden and crisp up.

To serve, scoop the ice cream into bowls. Give each person an espresso and tuiles on the side, and allow them to pour the coffee over in their own way.

This one is a proper autumnal dessert. The slight spice from the crumble matched with the pears and the caramel cream is comfort food at its very best. The poached pears and crumble will both keep well for a couple of weeks and can be used for a number of dishes or just to snack on when the mood takes you.

Caramel cream
WITH POACHED PEARS & GINGER CRUMBLE

SERVES 8

FOR THE GINGER CRUMBLE
150g unsalted butter
1 teaspoon ground ginger
250g plain flour, sifted
50g light muscovado sugar
100g caster sugar

FOR THE POACHED PEARS
350ml white wine
250g caster sugar
1 teaspoon vanilla seeds
   (scraped from ½ vanilla pod)
1 star anise
1 bay leaf
zest and juice of 1 lemon
4 pears, peeled

FOR THE CARAMEL CREAM
150g caster sugar
600ml double cream
5½ sheets of platinum-grade
   gelatine, soaked in water
   for 5 minutes
175ml whole milk
1 pinch of sea salt

Preheat the oven to 180°C/160°C/Gas Mark 4.

Make the crumble mixture. In a mixing bowl, using your fingertips rub together the butter, ground ginger and flour until it resembles breadcrumbs. Then add both sugars and mix through. Place the crumble on to a lined baking tray and bake for 15–20 minutes, giving it an occasional stir during cooking, until evenly coloured and cooked through. Remove from the oven and leave to cool. When cooled, crush into pieces, as you wish, and set aside. (You can do this in advance and keep in an airtight container until needed, if you like.)

For the poached pears, place all the ingredients, apart from the pears, in a saucepan with 350ml water over a medium heat. Bring to the boil, then reduce the heat to a low simmer. Add the pears and cook for 5–15 minutes – the exact time will depend how ripe they are – until tender to the point of a knife, but giving a little resistance. Scoop out the pears into a suitable container and pour over the poaching liquid. Allow to cool, then cover with cling film and refrigerate until ready to serve – you can serve them the day of poaching, but they are better the following day.

For the caramel cream, place the sugar in a large saucepan over a low heat. Allow to melt until you have a good, golden brown (or a little darker) caramel. Little by little, whisk in the cream, taking care as it may bubble up and spit at the start. Whisk well between each addition to prevent lumps, then once you have added all the cream, squeeze out the gelatine and add it to the pan along with the salt. Whisk to combine, then remove from the heat, pour in the milk and whisk again to combine. Pass the caramel through a sieve into a bowl and leave to cool slightly. Pour the caramel equally into your serving bowls and place in the fridge to set for at least 2–3 hours, but ideally overnight.

To serve, remove the pears from their soaking liquid (you can re-use the liquid for poaching another batch of pears, or other fruit such as plums, apricots or rhubarb) and quarter and core them. Top each bowl of cream with equal amounts of the pear quarters and finish with a good amount of ginger crumble.

This is a gem of a cheesecake recipe and quite unusual in technique. It is baked in the classic way to give all the desired flavours but is then re-blended so that it sets smooth with the base gently rolled into the cheesecake. Whisky isn't essential but is always a good addition.

White chocolate & whisky cheesecake
WITH ORANGE & HONEYCOMB

SERVES 10

FOR THE CHEESECAKE
210g white chocolate
600g full-fat cream cheese
2 eggs
1 egg yolk
125g caster sugar
25ml whisky

FOR THE BISCUIT CRUMB
150g porridge oats
200g wholemeal flour
1 pinch of salt
80g demerara sugar
1 teaspoon baking powder
140g unsalted butter, melted
1 egg, beaten

FOR THE HONEYCOMB
100g caster sugar
30g golden syrup
110g liquid glucose
10g bicarbonate of soda, sifted

FOR THE ORANGE PURÉE
5 oranges
400g caster sugar, plus 25g for
    coating the orange halves

Preheat the oven to 160°C/140°C fan/Gas Mark 2–3.

For the cheesecake, melt the white chocolate in a bowl set over a pan of simmering water (don't let the base of the bowl touch the water). Remove from the heat and scrape into a food processor. Add the cream cheese, eggs, egg yolk and sugar and blitz until smooth. Pour the mixture into a lined, medium-sized (about 35 x 24cm) baking tray and bake for 25–30 minutes, until the cheesecake has taken on a bit of colour and is set – it will crack and split (it doesn't look great at this point, but that's fine). Remove from the oven and leave to cool slightly. Transfer the cheesecake to the clean bowl of a food processor, add the whisky and blitz until smooth. Transfer to a lined tart case (we used a 35 x 11cm rectangular one, but a 15cm diameter round one would work, too) and refrigerate for 3–5 hours to set.

Increase the oven temperature to 180°C/160°C fan/Gas Mark 4.

For the biscuit crumb, add the oats to a large mixing bowl with the flour, salt, sugar and baking powder and mix well. Add the melted butter and the egg and bring the mixture together to form a crumble. (You're going to blitz it after baking, so don't worry too much about what it looks like now.) Line a baking tray with a silicone mat or sheet of baking paper and spread over the crumble. Bake for 15–20 minutes, until everything is evenly cooked. Remove from the oven and leave to cool completely. Transfer the mixture to a food process and blitz to a crumb (or crush it by hand, if you prefer). Set aside.

While the crumble is baking, make the honeycomb – work quickly, speed is of the essence! Line a small, deep baking tray or cake tin with low sides with baking paper. Put the sugar, golden syrup and glucose in a large saucepan over a medium heat. Warm the mixture until it reaches 165–170°C on a sugar thermometer, or it's a light golden caramel colour. Remove from the heat and quickly stir in the bicarbonate of soda – be very careful as the mixture will expand and bubble up. Pour the mixture into the lined tray (taking care not to get any on your skin) and leave somewhere safe for at least 20 minutes to cool and harden up.

For the orange purée, halve 2 of the oranges. Sprinkle the extra 25g of sugar on to a saucer and dip in all 4 halves, cut-sides downwards. Transfer the halves into a saucepan, sugared-sides downwards, over a medium heat and burn the oranges until properly blackened (you may want to watch out for the smoke detector as it will get smoky). Add 100ml of water to the pan to deglaze it and remove it from the heat. Leave to cool, then, using your hands, squeeze all the juice from the oranges into the pan and drain off all the liquid, keeping it to the side.

Halve the remaining oranges and cut them into thin slices. Place the slices a medium saucepan and just cover with water. Place over a medium heat and bring to the boil. Boil for 2 minutes, then drain the orange slices in a colander, discarding the liquid, and return the orange slices to the pan. Cover in cold water again and repeat the process 4 more times. The last time, add the 400g of sugar to the pan, bring to the boil and allow the liquid to reduce a little, until syrupy. Drain the orange slices, reserving the liquid.

Put the drained orange slices in a food processor with the burnt orange liquid. Blitz, adding the reserved orange syrup liquid, until you have a smooth purée (you may not need all the liquid). Leave to cool.

To serve, spread the biscuit crumb over a baking tray. Cut the cheesecake into portions and roll each portion in the crumb, then transfer to a serving plate. Drizzle over the orange purée and cover with a good amount of honeycomb.

Chocolate, peanut butter and jelly! This unexpected completely delicious combination came about as a result of an experiment to create a decadent vegan dessert that people might not realise was vegan. You can use any dairy replacement milk, but I use oat milk.

Chocolate ganache
WITH PEANUT BUTTER & RASPBERRY JELLY

SERVES 8

FOR THE GANACHE
250g caster sugar
1 pinch of sea salt
500ml oat milk
400g 70% dark chocolate,
    broken up
50ml first-press rapeseed oil

FOR THE PEANUT BUTTER TOPPING
225g smooth peanut butter
75g coconut oil

FOR THE RASPBERRY JELLY
500g frozen raspberries
50g caster sugar, plus extra for
    the carrageenan iota
5g carrageenan iota, or use 3
    leaves of platinum-grade gelatine
    soaked in water for 5 minutes

TO SERVE
100g raw peanuts
1 punnet of raspberries
    (about 250g)

For the ganache, line some small tart rings with cling film. Heat the sugar in a medium pan over a medium heat for 5 minutes, until it has formed a caramel. Add a pinch of sea salt and gradually add the oat milk about 100ml at a time – watch out as it will bubble up and be very hot – letting each batch combine into the caramel before adding the next. Repeat until you are left with a smooth, caramel milk. Whisk in the chocolate until melted, then transfer the mixture to a food processor. Blend on a medium speed, adding the rapeseed oil through the feed tube to combine. Pour the mixture equally into the moulds, leaving enough space at the top for the peanut butter topping. Place in the fridge for at least 1 hour to set.

While the ganache is setting, toast the peanuts to serve. Preheat the oven to 190°C/170°C fan/Gas Mark 5. Scatter the peanuts in a baking tray and bake for 12–15 minutes, or until toasted. Remove from the oven and leave to cool completely. Place in a food processor and blitz to a crumb (don't over-blitz or you will end up with paste). Set aside until ready to serve.

For the peanut butter topping, place the peanut butter and coconut oil in a bowl set over a pan of simmering water (don't let the base of the bowl touch the water). Whisk to emulsify, then pour the mixture equally into the moulds on top of the set ganache (the ganache must be set when you do this).

Make the raspberry jelly. Put the frozen raspberries in a large bowl with the sugar and cover with cling film. Set the bowl over a pan of simmering water (don't let the bowl touch the water) and leave over a low heat for 20–30 minutes to leach the liquid from the berries. Remove the bowl from the pan and leave, still covered, for a further 30 minutes. Strain the liquid from the berries – you should have about 500ml. If you're short, top it up with water; if you have too much, increase the carrageenan iota in the next step.

Whisk the carrageenan iota into a small amount of sugar. Pour the raspberry liquid into a medium pan and place over a low heat. Whisk in the carrageenan iota mixture, or squeeze out the gelatine and whisk it in, and heat the liquid to 80°C. Simmer for 3 minutes, then pour the liquid through a sieve into a container and refrigerate until set, preferably overnight.

To serve, remove each ganache from its mould on to a serving plate. Spoon on the jelly, top with the fresh raspberries and finish with the peanut crumb.

This is a jelly and cream dish for adults. The fino sherry pairs really well with the panna cotta giving a not too sweet alcohol hit. The set on the jelly is perfect, enabling you to turn them out with ease and achieve the perfect tight wobble. The prunes will keep well in the fridge and match well with porridge or yoghurt, or even as a pairing with roast pork.

Vanilla panna cotta
WITH SHERRY JELLY & SOAKED PRUNES

SERVES 6

FOR THE SHERRY JELLY
150ml Palo Cortado sherry
100g caster sugar
¾ sheet of platinum-grade
   gelatine soaked in 50ml of
   water for 5 minutes

FOR THE SOAKED PRUNES
pared peel and juice of
   1 unwaxed orange
50g caster sugar
1 teaspoon vanilla seeds (scraped
   from ½ vanilla pod)
1 star anise
200g prunes, pitted
1 Earl Grey tea bag

FOR THE PANNA COTTA
600ml double cream
175ml whole milk
125g caster sugar
¾ sheet of platinum-grade gelatine
   soaked in water for 5 minutes

You'll need 6 x 175ml dariole
   moulds or mini pudding basins

Start with the jelly. Pour 300ml of water into a saucepan and add the sherry and sugar. Place over a low heat and warm until the mixture reaches about 60°C on a sugar thermometer – you want it warm enough to melt the gelatine, but you don't want it to boil, as that would evaporate the alcohol. Remove from the heat. Squeeze out the gelatine from its soaking water and whisk it into the sherry mixture until dissolved. Pass the mixture through a sieve then pour equally into your chosen moulds. Refrigerate to set (at least 1 hour).

While the jelly is setting, make the prunes. Put the orange peel and juice in a medium saucepan with the sugar, vanilla, star anise, prunes, tea bag and 500ml of water. Place over a medium heat and bring to the boil. Reduce the heat and gently simmer for 5 minutes, until the peel has slightly softened, then remove from the heat, cover and leave to cool. Remove the tea bag (you can leave the other aromatics) and transfer to a suitable container to store in the fridge until you're ready to use.

Make the panna cotta. Heat the cream, milk and caster sugar in a pan over a medium heat, until the mixture reaches 60°C on a sugar thermometer. Squeeze out the gelatine from its soaking water and whisk it into the cream mixture until dissolved. Pass the mixture through a sieve into a bowl and set aside to cool completely (it must be completely cooled, otherwise you'll melt the jelly when you pour it on top and you won't get perfect layers).

Make sure the jelly is set in the moulds. Pour the cooled panna cotta equally on top of each jelly layer. Return the moulds to the fridge for at least a further 8–12 hours, before serving.

To serve, dip each mould for a second or two into a bowl of boiling water to release the sides, then invert on to a serving plate. Repeat for all the moulds. Serve the prunes, in their soaking liquid, alongside for people to help themselves.

On a trip to France with my family many years ago we visited a small family bistro where an outrageously decadent dessert called Lesley's Brownie was starring on the menu – we talk about those brownies to this day. This my homage to Lesley's brownies – totally over the top rich and sweet, chocolatey, nutty and just about everything you could want from a dessert.

Chocolate, clotted cream fudge brownie
WITH CRANBERRIES, HAZELNUTS & CLOTTED CREAM

SERVES 12

FOR THE FUDGE
135g caster sugar
50g golden syrup
120g clotted cream

FOR THE CANDIED HAZELNUTS
200g caster sugar
100g blanched hazelnuts
1 litre cooking oil, for frying
1 pinch of sea salt

FOR THE DRUNKEN CRANBERRIES
100g dried cranberries
200ml white wine

FOR THE BROWNIE
300g unsalted butter
300g 70% dark chocolate,
  broken into pieces
1 pinch of salt
5 eggs
400g caster sugar
200g plain flour, sifted
200g clotted cream or vanilla ice
  cream, to serve

Make the fudge. Line a 33 x 23cm baking tray with baking paper. Place all the fudge ingredients in a medium saucepan over a medium heat and bring the temperature up to 118°C on a sugar thermometer. Remove from the heat, transfer to the lined baking tray and leave to cool. Refrigerate to harden, then cut up the fudge into little pieces (small enough to go into the brownie, like fudge chips) and set aside.

Next, make the candied hazelnuts. Put the sugar in a saucepan with 200ml of water and place over a high heat. Bring to a simmer and add the nuts. Allow the liquid to reach 108°C on a sugar thermometer, then remove from the heat and drain the hazelnuts in a sieve.

Pour the cooking oil into a deep pan until two-thirds full and heat the oil to 180°C on a cooking thermometer or until a cube of day-old bread turns golden in 60 seconds (or preheat a deep-fat fryer to 180°C). Place the drained hazelnuts into the oil for about 90 seconds, until golden brown. Remove and drain on a baking tray lined with a clean J-cloth. Season with a pinch of sea salt and set aside.

Make the drunken cranberries. Place the cranberries in a small saucepan and add the wine. If the wine doesn't quite cover the cranberries, top up with water. Place over a low heat and simmer for 5 minutes, then remove from the heat and cover with a lid. Leave to soak for 30 minutes. Transfer the cranberries and the soaking water to a suitable container and refrigerate until needed.

Make the brownie. Preheat the oven to 180°C/160°C fan/Gas Mark 4 and line a 33 x 23cm baking tray with baking paper.

Place the butter and chocolate together with the pinch of salt in a bowl and place it over a pan of simmering water (don't let the base of the bowl touch the water). Meanwhile, in a separate bowl, whisk together the eggs and

...method continued on page 244

sugar, until light and frothy. Pour the butter and chocolate mixture into the eggs-and-sugar mixture and whisk to combine. Fold in the sifted flour until no streaks remain.

Pour the mixture into the prepared baking tin. Push about 10–12 chunks of the fudge into the brownie, distributing the fudge evenly, then bake for 20–25 minutes, or until the top of the brownie has cracked a little. Remove from the oven and allow to cool until warm.

To serve, cut the brownie into good-sized portions and place each portion on a serving plate. Top with the candied hazelnuts and drunken cranberries. Finish with a good spoonful of clotted cream or ice cream.

This is a very adult trifle – sweet jelly and bay leaf-flavoured custard mixed with the tartness of blackcurrants. In the restaurant we make our own sponge but shop-bought ladyfingers would work perfectly and in their own way are very special.

Pear & vermouth trifle
WITH BAY LEAF CUSTARD, CREAM & BLACKCURRANTS

SERVES 12

FOR THE BLACKCURRANT CREAM
125g frozen blackcurrants
50g caster sugar
juice of ½ lemon
500ml double cream

FOR THE SPONGE
100g unsalted butter
110g golden syrup
110g dark brown soft sugar
75g stem ginger, finely grated
1½ pears, peeled and grated
　(eat the other half)
160g plain flour, sifted
½ teaspoon bicarbonate of soda
¼ teaspoon baking powder
About 75ml sweet vermouth,
　for soaking the sponge

FOR THE JELLY
1 litre pear juice
7 sheets of platinum-grade gelatine
　soaked in water for 5 minutes

Make a blackcurrant compote for the blackcurrant cream. Place the blackcurrants in a medium saucepan with the sugar and lemon juice. Cook over a medium heat for about 10 minutes, until softened and jammy. The liquid will leach from the fruit, and the mixture will turn wet – keep cooking and stirring for about 10 minutes, until it reduces to the right consistency. Remove from the heat and set aside.

For the sponge, line a 27 x 20cm baking or brownie tin (3cm deep) and preheat the oven to 190°C/170°C fan/Gas Mark 5.

Put the butter, golden syrup and sugar in a small saucepan over a low heat. Allow to melt. Meanwhile, put the grated stem ginger and pears in a large mixing bowl and, when ready, add the melted butter mixture. Whisk to combine. Sift in the flour, bicarbonate of soda and baking powder and stir until no streaks remain. Pour the batter into the prepared tin and bake for 20–25 minutes, until a skewer inserted into the centre comes out clean. Set aside to cool.

Cut the sponge to fit the glasses for your individual trifles. Place a layer of sponge in the bottom of each glass. Brush the tops of the sponges with the vermouth – use as much as you like, to taste. Set aside.

For the jelly, pour the pear juice into a medium pan over a low heat. Warm gently until it reaches 60°C on a sugar thermometer. Squeeze the excess water from the gelatine and add it to the pan with the pear juice. Whisk to combine until the gelatine has dissolved, then pass the liquid through a sieve into a bowl and allow to cool slightly. Pour the jelly equally into each serving glass to form a layer about the same depth as the sponge. Refrigerate to set (about 2 hours).

For the custard, whisk the egg yolks and sugar together in a bowl and sift the flours together into a separate bowl. Set aside. In a large saucepan

...ingredients & method continued on page 246

FOR THE CUSTARD
2 egg yolks
50g caster sugar
10g plain flour
10g cornflour
250ml whole milk
about 1 teaspoon vanilla seeds
    (scraped from ½ vanilla pod)
1 bay leaf

You'll need 12 individual serving
    glasses (about 300ml each)
    for your trifles

heat the milk with the vanilla seeds and bay leaf over a medium heat until it comes to the boil. Remove the bay leaf and slowly, little by little, pour the infused milk into the bowl with the egg mixture, whisking well. When all the milk has been incorporated, whisk the wet mixture into the bowl with the flour, adding the custard little by little and making sure there are no lumps. Return the mixture to the saucepan and whisk over a low heat until thickened and the flour has cooked out. Remove from the heat and leave to cool to room temperature. Cover the surface of the custard with cling film to prevent a skin forming and refrigerate for 1 hour or so to cool completely.

When the custard is fully chilled, remove it from the fridge, uncover and give it a whisk, then spoon it on top of the set jelly layers. Return the trifles to the fridge until you're ready to serve.

To finish the trifles, whisk the double cream to just under soft peaks. Fold in the blackcurrant compote to ripple it through the cream. Spoon equal amounts of the blackcurrant cream on to the custard layer of each trifle and serve straight away.

Why mess with perfection? This British classic is often on the Root menu over winter.
Regular clotted cream is a perfectly acceptable alternative to the ice cream version.

You can make the sticky toffee pudding as traybake. Use a 30 x 22cm baking tray and
bake for 25–30 minutes, until a skewer comes out clean. You can also make the individual
puddings (or traybake) in advance and reheat in a microwave or steamer to serve.

Sticky toffee pudding
WITH TOFFEE SAUCE & CLOTTED CREAM ICE CREAM

SERVES 6–8

**FOR THE CLOTTED CREAM
ICE CREAM**
200g caster sugar
12 egg yolks
500ml whole milk
1 tablespoon glucose
500g clotted cream

FOR THE PUDDING
250g pitted dates
1 small pinch of salt
250g demerara sugar
75g unsalted butter, softened,
    plus extra for greasing
1 teaspoon golden syrup
250g self-raising flour
3 eggs
1½ teaspoons bicarbonate of soda

FOR THE TOFFEE SAUCE
225ml double cream
225g dark brown soft or dark
    muscovado sugar
150g unsalted butter
pinch of sea salt

You'll need 12 x 175ml dariole
    moulds or mini pudding basins

First, make the ice cream. Combine the sugar and egg yolks in a bowl and
whisk well. Place the milk and glucose in a medium saucepan over a medium
heat and bring to the boil. Add the clotted cream and whisk to incorporate.
Slowly pour the cream mixture into the egg yolk mix, whisking to make sure
the egg yolks don't scramble. Add the mixture back to the pan and place
over a low heat, stirring continuously. Bring the temperature up to 80°C
on a sugar thermometer and remove from the heat. Transfer to a container,
leave to cool, then refrigerate until completely chilled (about 1 hour).

Transfer the cold mixture to an ice-cream machine and churn until set.
Scrape into a container and store in the freezer until needed. Leave the ice
cream to soften in the fridge for a few minutes before serving, if necessary.

Make the pudding. Preheat the oven to 180°C/160°C fan/Gas Mark 4.
Lightly grease your moulds. Put the dates, salt and 400ml water in a medium
saucepan over a medium heat. Bring to the boil, then remove from the heat
and cover with a lid. Leave the dates to soften like this for 5 minutes.

In a large bowl, cream together the sugar and the softened butter using a
hand whisk, until light and fluffy. Add the golden syrup and sift in the flour.
Fold them in until the mixture is fully combined. Add the eggs, then the
dates, including their soaking liquid, and the bicarbonate of soda and whisk
with a hand whisk to form a light batter. Pour the batter equally into the
prepared moulds, filling each two-thirds of the way up the sides, leaving
room for the puddings to rise. Place the moulds in a baking tray and bake for
25–30 minutes, or until a skewer inserted into the centres comes out clean.
Remove from the oven and leave until cool enough to handle.

While the puddings are baking, make the toffee sauce. Place all the sauce
ingredients in a medium saucepan over a low heat and bring to a light boil.
Whisk to combine, set aside and keep warm.

To serve, invert the puddings out of the moulds into individual serving
bowls. Pour over a good amount of the warm sauce and finish with a
good scoop of the ice cream. Serve immediately.

You should be able to source some carrot-shaped cutters online for these jellies, in which case they will not only taste great but also look pretty. If you want a bit of fizz in your jellies, then just add a little citric acid to the sugar when you roll them.

Carrot jellies

MAKES ABOUT 24

12g powdered pectin
400g caster sugar, plus an
    extra 50g for rolling
500ml carrot juice
120g liquid glucose
parsley or chervil powder
    (see page 271), to garnish

Line a 28 x 20cm baking tray with a double layer of cling film.

Mix the pectin in a small bowl with 50g of the sugar. Set aside.

Pour the carrot juice into a medium saucepan, place over a medium heat and bring to the boil. Whisk in the pectin and sugar mixture, then add the remaining sugar and the glucose. Bring the temperature to 108°C on a sugar thermometer, then remove from the heat and pass the mixture through a sieve into the prepared baking tray.

Leave the jelly to cool to room temperature, then refrigerate to cool and set completely (about 2–3 hours, maybe longer).

Remove the set jelly from the tray on to a chopping board and, using a knife, cut it into 24 equal portions (or, if you have a carrot-shaped cutter, use that!).

Place the 50g of sugar over a plate. Roll the jellies in the sugar, then dip the top of each into the parsley or chervil powder (to represent the green tops of a carrot). Serve straight away.

When we first opened Root we kept a small freezer downstairs and would find ourselves running up and down outside every time an order came into the kitchen. Now we have the luxury of a freezer squeezed into our small kitchen and can make a large number of ice creams and sorbets ready to have to hand.

This is the master base for all our ice creams, into which we blend whatever flavours or folds we want. We started off by just making the classics and then we began to introduce some crazy new flavours and now we tend to use whatever is left over after we've changed the dessert menu. It's a great no-waste way of cooking and the results usually taste amazing.

Here are some of our flavours. We pour the hot base over some, like the cakes, and others we churn and then fold through the ingredients, as in our cherry ripple.

Ice-cream master base

MAKES 2 LITRES

1 litre whole milk
800ml double cream
1 vanilla pod, or 1 teaspoon
vanilla seeds (scraped from
½ a vanilla pod)
24 egg yolks (about 480g)
360g caster sugar

To make the ice-cream base, place the milk, cream and vanilla in a large saucepan over a medium heat and slowly bring to a simmer (but don't let it boil).

While the milk is coming to a simmer, place the egg yolks and caster sugar into a large bowl and whisk until light and fluffy.

As soon as the milk mixture is simmering, remove it from the heat and, little by little, pour it into the egg mixture, whisking continuously as you do so (it can help if someone else is pouring as you whisk). Once the mixture is combined, return it to the saucepan and place it back on the low heat. Using a wooden spoon or spatula, stir the mixture for about 5–8 minutes, until it thickens enough to coat the back of the spoon. Remove from the heat and pour into a bowl or other container to cool down slightly, then cover and refrigerate to chill completely (about 1–2 hours).

Transfer the chilled ice-cream base to an ice-cream machine and churn until set. Scrape into a suitable container and store in the freezer until needed. Transfer the ice cream to the fridge for a few minutes to soften up before serving, if necessary.

Except for the coffee ice cream, you can make any of the following flavourings (all of them among our favourites) by folding the extra ingredients into the ice-cream base after churning and before you transfer the ice cream to the freezer to firm up completely.

To make the coffee ice cream, add the coffee beans, espresso shots and liqueur to the milk and cream mixture at the start of the process, then continue as for the remaining base method on page 252.

Flavouring your ice cream

Chocolate cake – add a handful of crumbled chocolate cake and 4 tablespoons cocoa powder.

Pumpkin – add 100g pumpkin purée and 1 tablespoon ground ginger or cinnamon.

Rocky roads – add a handful each of fudge, raisins, biscuits and nuts.

Eton mess – add 5 tablespoons strawberry purée and a handful of broken-up meringue.

Cherry ripple – add a handful of pitted cherries and 5 tablespoons cherry purée.

Lemon meringue – add 5 tablespoons lemon curd and a handful of broken-up meringue.

Carrot cake – add a handful of crumbled carrot cake and 5 tablespoons carrot jam.

Rum baba and raisin – add a handful of crumbled rum babas and a handful of soaked raisins.

Christmas pudding – add a handful of mincemeat or crumbled Christmas pudding.

Apple pie – add 5 tablespoons apple compote and a handful of crumble.

Coffee ice cream – add 2 espresso shots, 30g crushed coffee beans and 2 shots of coffee liqueur.

All of these recipes are here to help make your life easier in the kitchen. They are the essential base recipes that will get used time and time again and are good to keep in the fridge ready for when a recipe demands them. They will all keep well if properly stored.

larder

Focaccia or flat breads

MAKES 1 LOAF OR 14 FLAT BREADS

450g strong white bread flour
50g semolina
30g onion seeds (optional)
15g fresh yeast
280ml lukewarm water
100ml rapeseed oil, plus 1
  tablespoon for sprinkling
  the focaccia
12g salt

TO FINISH THE FOCACCIA
a few rosemary or thyme sprigs,
  leaves picked
sea salt

Put the flour in the bowl of an electric stand mixer fitted with the dough hook. Add the semolina, onion seeds (if using) and fresh yeast. Turn on the mixer at a low speed.

Combine the water and rapeseed oil in a jug. With the mixer running, pour the wet ingredients into the dry, then add the salt. Increase the speed to medium and mix for 10–15 minutes, until the dough is smooth and coming away from the sides of the bowl.

Turn out the dough on to a clean work surface and work it into a large, smooth ball. Then, transfer the dough to a lightly oiled bowl, cover with a cloth and leave at room temperature to rise for about 45 minutes, or until the dough has doubled in size (the exact time this takes will depend on the ambient temperature in the room).

If you're making flat breads: Divide the dough into 14 equally sized pieces (each should weigh about 70g). Shape into balls, then transfer them to a lightly oiled or semolina-dusted baking tray, cover with a lid or cling film to prevent a skin forming, then leave to prove for 30 minutes, until more than doubled in size.

Heat a griddle to hot or place a frying pan on a medium–high heat and allow to heat up.

Press each flat bread into a mini-pizza shape and place the bread under the grill or in the pan. Cook for 2 minutes on each side, until nicely puffed up and golden.

If you're making focaccia: Heat the oven to 240°C/220°C fan/Gas Mark 8. Tip out the dough on to a lightly floured work surface and use your hands to knock it back, until smooth. Place it into a well-oiled baking tray (measuring about 33 x 23cm) or a large loaf tin, flattening it out and stretching it towards the edges and corners. Cover with a cloth and leave to prove for 30 minutes, until more than doubled in size. Sprinkle over the herbs, sea salt and a little oil, then bake for 25 minutes, until golden and the base sounds hollow when removed from the tin and tapped.

Pakoras!

		x 4
125g	Self Raise Flour	500 g
190g	Plain Flour	760 g
2 tsp	Cumin Seeds	8 tsp
1 tsp	ground Coriander	4 tsp
1/2 tsp	Chilli Powder	1 tsp
2 tsp	Turmeric	8 tsp
2	Egg Yolks	
Pinch	fresh Coriander	
15 x	Small onions sliced	4 x bunch
1 x	Large Cauli	4 x head
2 x tbsp	onion seeds	8 tbsp
approx	250 ml Water	1 litre
1 tsp	Curry oil	

SESAME CRACKER

500g	BUTTER → Buere noisette
500g	FLOUR
150g	BLACK SESAME
150g	WHITE SESAME
600ml	BEER → OJ
	SALT
150g	SUGAR

We use this brilliant brine when cooking particular cuts so as to help season deep into the meat. It's handy to have in the kitchen and is easy to make. This is the base recipe but depending on what you are brining, the aromatics used can change to suit taste and cut. For example, if you are bringing a chicken you might want to add some lemon and thyme, or if it's a meat at Christmas, you could add cloves and oranges.

Brine

MAKES 4 LITRES

300g table salt
200g caster sugar
6 peppercorns
2 bay leaves
pared peel of 1 unwaxed lemon
2 thyme sprigs

Simply add all the ingredients to a saucepan with 3 litres of water. Give it a whisk and bring to the boil. Allow to boil and whisk until the salt and sugar has dissolved, then remove from the heat and leave to cool. Use according to the recipe method.

Just like vegetable stock, we keep pickle liquid in the restaurant kitchen at all times ready to go. This is our base pickle recipe. You can tailor the pickle as you wish, adding extra flavourings such as citrus peels, spices or aromatics. Make a large amount to keep in the fridge for use as the occasion demands.

Pickle liquid

MAKES ABOUT 1 LITRE

600ml white wine vinegar
400ml caster sugar
300ml white wine

Place the ingredients in a saucepan with 300ml of water. Whisk them together and place them over a medium heat. Bring to the boil, then immediately remove from the heat. Leave the liquid to cool, transfer it to an airtight container and keep refrigerated until you're ready to use.

I'm pretty relaxed as to what to put into a vegetable stock and am happy to use up whatever trimmings I have around the kitchen. Tops of leeks, shallot ends, fennel tops, parsley stalks – collect the trimmings over a couple of days of cooking and you will have yourself the makings of a vegetable stock ready to go. Onions, celery, carrots, leeks, celeriac, fennel and mushrooms are all great but keep away from vegetable peelings, onion skins and vegetables such as turnip, courgette, potatoes and cabbage. Make sure the vegetables are washed and clean before using.

Vegetable stock

MAKES ABOUT 2 LITRES

leftover vegetables or vegetable trimmings, such as 2 onions, 1 leek top, 1 fennel, 2 celery sticks, 1 carrot and parsley stalks
aromatics, (peppercorns, fennel seeds or bay leaf are a good start)
1 glass of white wine (optional)

Place the roughly chopped vegetables or cuttings into a saucepan and cover with 2 litres of water. Add your chosen aromatics, and if you have some white wine spare, then add that, too.

Place the pan over a high heat and bring to the boil. Reduce the heat and simmer for 10 minutes, until infused. Remove from the heat, cover with a lid and leave the stock to cool. Strain the stock into a bowl, discarding the contents of the sieve. Pour the stock into an airtight container and refrigerate until needed.

This is a classic sharp salad dressing that we use with many of our dishes served at Root. Good with vegetables cooked on the grill, for salads, for finishing certain dishes or simply as the mood and the ingredient to hand takes you. Use a good-quality vinegar!

Salad dressing

MAKES ABOUT 500ML

75ml chardonnay or other good-quality white wine vinegar
1 tablespoon Dijon mustard
200ml cooking oil
50ml rapeseed oil

Pour the vinegar into a food processor and add the mustard. With the processor working on full speed, add the oil through the feed tube. Process until the mixture fully emulsifies and the dressing is thick and creamy. Transfer to an airtight container and refrigerate until needed.

Alternatively, make the dressing in a bowl: whisk the vinegar and mustard together in the bowl and add the oil, whisking all the time. The results will be less emulsified than you get in a food processor – more of a vinaigrette – and the mixture will split once you store it. Just give it a shake or a whisk again to recombine before using.

CK PEPPER

CORIANDER

NTHAM

CUMIN

WHITE PEPPER

NUTMEG

ONION SEED

ALLSPICE

CARAWAY

MACE

AKING POWDER
BICARB
SPICEY ONION
STAR ANISE
CHILLI
CAYENNE
CURRY POWDER

Seaweed vinegar

MAKES 1 LITRE

500ml white wine vinegar
200ml white wine
150g caster sugar
6 sheets of dried nori or
   various dried seaweed

Place all the ingredients in a large saucepan with 300ml of water and place over a high heat. Bring to the boil, then reduce the heat to a simmer and cook for 5 minutes. Remove from the heat, cover with a lid and set aside to cool.

Once cool, strain the vinegar through a fine sieve lined with a muslin cloth into a jug. Transfer to an airtight container and refrigerate until needed.

Elderflower vinegar

MAKES 1 LITRE

500ml white wine vinegar
200ml white wine
100g caster sugar
30 freshly picked elderflower
   heads, picked over to remove
   any bugs or dirt

Place all the ingredients apart from the elderflower into a large saucepan with 300ml of water and place over a high heat. Bring to the boil, then reduce the heat to a simmer and cook for 5 minutes. Remove from the heat and add the elderflower heads. Cover with a lid and set aside to cool.

Once cool, strain the vinegar through a fine sieve lined with a muslin cloth into a jug. Transfer to an airtight container and refrigerate until needed.

We have a little cold smoker at the restaurant. Cold smokers are actually not that expensive and they are fun to play around with. We use ours for all sorts of things – smoked oils, sauces and butter, and this smoked yoghurt among them. There's no need for a smoker to create smoked yoghurt at home, though; you can follow this recipe below.

Smoked yoghurt

MAKES ABOUT 450G

a large pinch of sea salt
500g yoghurt
50ml smoked rapeseed oil

All you need to do is to salt and hang the yoghurt in a muslin cloth placed in a sieve over a large bowl for 2–3 hours.

Whisk in the oil, or as much as gives you that smoky flavour coming through. The recipe is easily scaled up, and keeps in the fridge for up to 5 days.

Use the yoghurt as a dip with bread or alongside a fish dish or some lamb.

Our chef Josh Gibbons brought this fantastic recipe with him when he joined us and it's been used with most things imaginable ever since. In the book I've used it with the celeriac dish on page 26 and the chicken recipe on page 210, but don't stop there and be free to use it as you wish.

Dredge

MAKES ABOUT 500G

400g strong white bread flour
    or gluten-free flour
40g corn flour
2g baking powder
6g garlic powder
8g onion powder
10g white pepper
6g smoked paprika
5g cayenne pepper
3g ground turmeric

Combine the ingredients in a large bowl, then transfer to an airtight container and store in a dry place. The dredge will keep for 6 months or more.

Making preserved lemons is time consuming so make a large batch and store them well as they will keep for a very long time and mature wonderfully. If done correctly and stored well they can be kept for months.

Preserved lemons

MAKES 3 X 500ML JARS

10 lemons, washed
250g sea salt
250g caster sugar

Preheat the oven to 160°C/140°C fan/Gas Mark 3. Sterilise the jars by washing them in hot water and rinsing them well. Place the jars on a baking tray and place in the oven for 10 minutes. Meanwhile, soak the lids in boiling water for a few minutes. Or, run the jars and the lids through the hottest cycle in your dishwasher and leave to air dry.

Carefully slice off the very top and very bottom of each lemon. Taking each lemon in turn, slice top to bottom lengthways through the middle, but without cutting all the way through – leaving the lemon intact at the base. Repeat the cut top to bottom as if you were slicing into quarters, but still leave the base intact.

Mix together the salt and sugar in a bowl and rub the mixture all over and into the lemons, making sure you pack it into the cut centres.

Place the lemons into your sterilised jar, really packing them in so that they are nice and tight. If there is any remaining salt and sugar mixture, pack it into the top of the jar, then seal with the lid. Place the jar in a dry, cool place and leave for 1 week.

After a week the lemons should have released enough liquid to fill the jar and cover the lemons themselves. If necessary, top up the jar with lemon juice to cover. (You may need to add a bit of baking paper and a little weight to hold down the lemons so that they are submerged.)

Return the jar to a cool, dry place and leave for another 10–12 weeks. The texture and colour will change and you will be left with lovely, intense lemons that you can slice down and use in cooking. Keep the lemons submerged in their liquid and store in the fridge for up to 6 months.

This nut-free, dairy-free pesto is a real crowd pleaser. It's great served with pasta, or drizzled over vegetables.

Kale pesto

MAKES 500G

100g kale
12 basil leaves
100g pumpkin seeds
1 garlic clove
1 roasted garlic bulb (see page
   267), flesh squeezed out
25ml sherry vinegar
250ml rapeseed oil
salt and freshly ground
   black pepper

Put all the ingredients into a food processor and blitz for 20 seconds, until the mixture resembles pesto. Make sure that all the ingredients have combined and blended well and check the seasoning. Transfer to an airtight container and store in the fridge until ready to use (it will keep for up to 5 days).

We use mayonnaise in a lot in our restaurant recipes and this version provides the base for them all. Feel free to change the oil (to seaweed or garlic, for example) to create different outcomes and you can add paste or purées (see the honey and mustard mayo on page 46, or try adding gochujang) to it to use in a variety of ways.

Mayonnaise

MAKES 1 SMALL JAR

35g Dijon mustard
30ml white wine vinegar
90g egg yolks (3 yolks)
a pinch of salt, plus extra to season
500ml cooking oil
1 tablespoon lemon juice,
   plus extra, to finish

Put the mustard, vinegar, egg yolks and salt into a bowl and whisk to combine. Slowly pour in the oil, whisking the whole time, until you have incorporated all the oil (you may find it easier if someone else holds the bowl for you; or use an electric stand mixer or food processor) and the mixture has emulsified. Whisk in the lemon juice and check the seasoning. Add a tablespoon of water if the mayonnaise is too thick (I like mine this way – like traditional French mayo – but you may prefer yours thinner). Finish with a little extra lemon juice and more salt to season, if needed.

This burnt onion purée is great to use in a variety of dishes, such as risottos, stews, sauces and gravies, having an intensely, dark, sweet flavour. The key to success is to cook over a high heat with a good amount of salt – you want that delicious roasted, caramelised onion flavour.

Burnt onion purée

MAKES 500G

6 onions, thinly sliced with
    a mandolin
4 tablespoons cooking oil
200ml white wine, cider,
    vegetable stock or water
1 tablespoon rapeseed oil
1 tablespoon sherry vinegar
sea salt

Sprinkle the onion slices with salt. Heat the cooking oil in a large saucepan over a medium heat. When hot, add the onions and cook for about 10–15 minutes, until softened and cooked down and starting to catch on the bottom of the pan. Keep cooking and stirring for a further 5 minutes, until the onions have darkened – you want them really caramelised, but not burnt (despite the name!).

Add the white wine, cider, vegetable stock or water and deglaze the pan, scraping up the stickiness from the base. Cook out the liquid until it has all gone (about 10 minutes), leaving you with soft onions.

Transfer the onions to a food processor and blend to a smooth purée. Add the rapeseed oil and vinegar, blend again, then taste and season. Transfer to an airtight container and refrigerate until needed.

It is Michelin starred chef and friend Josh Eggleton who is responsible for getting me irredeemably hooked on roasted garlic – it just seems to make so many already delicious things taste even better. Roast a decent number of bulbs at a time and keep them in the fridge so that they are always there when needed.

Roasted garlic

similar-sized whole garlic
    bulbs, unpeeled

Preheat the oven to 170°C/150°C fan/Gas Mark 3. Place the garlic bulbs in a roasting tin for about 30–35 minutes, depending on the size of the garlic, until the bulbs are soft to touch and some golden garlic juices are leaching from the bulb. Remove from the oven and leave to cool.

To use in a recipe, simply slice the top or the bottom off the garlic bulb and squeeze out the contents on to a saucer. Use the back of a knife to crush the pulp a little more, then simply add to whatever you're cooking.

Simple and classic and great to use with almost everything – vegetables, meat, fish or bread. It can be frozen so make a good batch.

Garlic butter

MAKES 500G

2 bunches of flat-leaf parsley, leaves picked
3 roasted garlic bulbs (see page 267), flesh squeezed out
1 large garlic clove, peeled
500g unsalted butter, softened at room temperature

Bring a pan of salted water to the boil. Have a bowl of iced water ready to go.

Plunge the flat-leaf parsley leaves into the boiling water for 90 seconds, then scoop them out with a slotted spoon and transfer them immediately to the iced water.

Using your hands, squeeze the excess water from the cooked parsley. Place it in a food processor with the roasted garlic flesh and garlic clove and blend to a paste. Add the softened butter and blend again until fully combined. Remove from the food processor and place in an airtight container in the fridge. The butter will keep for as long as the use-by date on the original butter. Delicious on garlic bread, baked fish, steak, and roasted vegetables – among much else.

In the restaurant we are lucky enough to have a Thermomix, which can heat as well as blend. We use this when creating our green oils, heating and blending at the same time, reaching the perfect temperature to keep each oil as green as possible. But, there are other ways to do this – this method tells you how.

Green/herb oils

MAKES 500ML

herb of choice for your oil, for example choose from 2 bunches of flat-leaf parsley, 3 bunches of dill, 3 bunches of chives, 3 bunches of basil, 250g leek tops, thinly sliced, 250g fennel tops or 6 sheets of nori seaweed, torn
500ml neutral-tasting oil, such as sunflower oil or vegetable oil

You can blanch your chosen herbs or greens in boiling water and then blend them into the oil, but the easiest way is to blend the raw herbs directly into the oil, using a blender or food processor. It takes a little longer than blanching first, but is less of a faff. As the motor in the blender runs, it heats up and heats the oil with it – enough so as to keep the oil green.

Remove the large stalks from the herbs and roughly chop the remainder to help with blending.

When you have blended the herbs into the oil, pass the mixture through a muslin or J-cloth into a bowl or jug. You will be left with a clear, flavoured green oil to use as you wish. (Some herbs contain a lot of moisture and that will collect at the bottom of the oil when it settles: strain this off if possible.)

In the summer, when there is a massive surplus of tomatoes, this is a great way of using the excess crop. You can scale up the recipe to make as much as you would like.

Dried tomatoes

MAKES 250G

2 bunches of vine cherry
   tomatoes, halved
2 thyme sprigs, leaves picked
   and chopped
1 garlic clove, crushed
rapeseed oil, for sprinkling
splash of sherry vinegar
sea salt and freshly ground
   black pepper

Heat your oven to its lowest setting.

Place the tomatoes, cut sides upwards, in a baking tray, sprinkle over the thyme leaves and garlic cloves and a little rapeseed oil and a splash of vinegar and season with salt and pepper.

Bake the tomatoes for about 2–3 hours, until they are about two-thirds of their original size (you can fully dry them out, but they do get pretty intense and tart).

The tomatoes will store in fridge for 1 week. Use them in salads and to add a flavour hit to sauces.

Onion powder is a great provider of background flavour in many dishes. It has a wonderful bitter-sweet flavour that makes anything and everything taste better. It keeps very well so make a large amount to be used as a staple in your cooking over the months ahead.
   At the restaurant we use a plate warmer to dry the onions, set at around 50–60°C, but popping the onions at the bottom of the oven on the lowest setting will work just as well.

Burnt onion powder

MAKES 100G

at least 6 onions,
   peeled and halved
pinch of sea salt

Slice the onions using a mandolin into very thin slices. Spread out the onion slices evenly over a baking tray and place the tray in the bottom of the oven. Leave the onions there for 12 hours until they are completely dried out, brittle and dark brown – some of the onions will take on more colour than others, but that just adds to the flavour. Place the dried onions in a food processor with the pinch of salt and blend to a powder. Pass the powder through a fine sieve into a container, then seal with the lid.

These herb powders are created in the same way as the onion powder, using a dehydrator or at the bottom of your oven on the lowest setting. Use at least two bunches of the herbs as the end result after drying will be quite small.

Parsley, chervil or leek powder

MAKES 25G

at least 2 bunches of parsley
   or chervil, leaves picked
4 leek tops
1 pinch of salt

For the parsley or chervil powder: Preheat the oven to its lowest setting. Place the parsley or chervil leaves on a baking tray and place them on the bottom shelf of the oven for at least 2 hours, until the leaves are dry and brittle, but still maintaining their colour.

For the leek powder: Preheat the oven to 200°C/180°C fan/Gas Mark 6. Slice the leek tops thinly, then place them in a baking tray and bake for 20 minutes, until almost blackened. Remove them from the oven and reduce the heat to the lowest setting. Return the leek tops to the lowest shelf and leave to dry for 2 hours, until really crisp and brittle.

Place the dried-out parsley, chervil or leek tops in a food processor with the pinch of salt and blend to a powder. Pass the powder through a fine sieve into a container and seal with the lid. Store in a dry place for up to 6 months.

Chefs all over the UK use wild garlic – probably one of the most identifiable and accessible foraged ingredients we have available to us. Like any plant, it has its stages of growth and they are all amazing for cooking with. The small, tender, young leaves are subtle and lovely to use just wilted slightly. When the plant grows larger, it develops a thicker, more textured leaf that needs more vigorous cooking and is perfect for turning into preserves, such as oils, ferments, vinegars or frozen purées. Wild garlic flowers are also delicious – use them in salads and to garnish dishes. Finally, after the flowers fall, the plant gives us green wild garlic seeds, which we call 'capers', because that's what they look like.

Pickled wild garlic capers

MAKES 1 MEDIUM-SIZED JAR

500g wild garlic capers
500ml brine (see page 258)
500ml pickle liquid (see page 258)

Remove the stalks from the garlic capers. Pour over enough brine to cover and leave them to soak overnight.

The following day, remove the garlic capers from the brine and place them in a clean, airtight jar. Cover them with pickle liquid and refrigerate until needed.

Use them to give you that hit of spring-like garlic all year round.

Pickled mustard seeds are good to add to any number of dishes and salads. They bring an amazing sweet spicy heat to a dish and once made they keep well in the fridge for up to a few months.

Pickled mustard seeds

MAKES 1 MEDIUM KILNER JAR

200g yellow mustard seeds
500g white wine vinegar
180g caster sugar

Put all the ingredients in a saucepan with 200ml of water over a high heat. Bring to the boil, then reduce the heat and simmer until the mixture has thickened and reduced so there is little liquid (about 15 minutes). The mustard seeds will swell and become juicy like big caviar. Leave to cool, then transfer to an airtight container and refrigerate until needed.

This recipe can be used for all nuts in both savoury dishes and desserts or just to snack. Finishing them with a pinch of sea salt is a nice touch. You will need to take extra care around the kitchen as a lot of very hot liquids are involved. Make sure that your fryer, or the oil in your pan, is preheated to 180°C.

Candied nuts

MAKES 250G NUTS

cooking oil, for frying
250g nuts of your choice
400g caster sugar

Pour the cooking oil into a deep pan until two-thirds full and heat to 180°C on a cooking thermometer or until a cube of day-old bread turns golden in 60 seconds (or preheat a deep-fat fryer to 180°C).

Place the nuts and sugar into a separate saucepan with 400ml of water and place over a high heat. Allow the sugar to dissolve and bring the temperature of the liquid up to 108°C on a sugar thermometer.

Place a colander over a bowl and pour the nuts into it, letting the liquid drain into the bowl. Now place the drained, coated nuts straight into the hot oil. Cook for about 1 minute until golden brown. Remove from the oil and allow to cool on a baking tray.

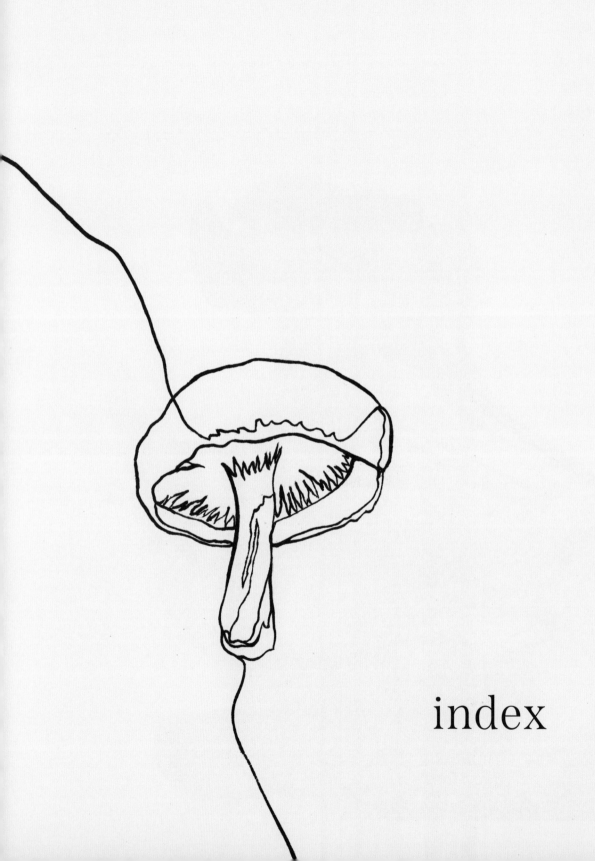

index

Thanks

This book is a true dream come true for me and a product of some amazing people. My name is on it but there should be so many more listed, as without them it would be nothing. The whole team at Absolute have been a pleasure to work with. First and foremost to Jon and Meg for giving me the opportunity to create this book and trusting me and what I envisioned. To Emily for the constant support and reassurance, and to Marie and Peter for the amazing design and layout of this book. The whole team couldn't have made me feel more comfortable in creating something I never thought I could. To Alex, your photography not only makes the book what it is, but you made the whole experience so enjoyable. To Will Freeman for your continued support and beautiful work, which has helped make Root what it is and finished off this book so perfectly. To Judy, who actually made my recipes make sense, also making it fun along the way. I am truly grateful to you all.

This is almost the most important part of the book for me, as with out any of these people it would not even have been possible. The most heartfelt thank you goes to my mum for putting us/me before everything, for teaching me the joys of cooking and always encouraging us. To dad, who I have learnt so much from, for teaching us about hard work and the importance of meals together, and for always making us eat around the table. Thanks for introducing us to France at a young age and all the joy it brought us. Luckily, I become more like my dad each day and I couldn't be prouder of that. To my older brother and sister who have always lead by example and shown me how it's done in life; I couldn't have asked for better role models. To Nanny Stark for passing on the cooking genes and Nanny for the quality cakes and Welsh cakes.

To my wife Megan, without whom Root would not be what it is; you are the backbone of not only the restaurant but also me. You are the kindest, honest, most hard-working, wonderful human being I know, and is such a joy to share my life with you.

To Josh Eggleton, whom I cannot thank enough for everything. I can honestly say I don't know where I would be without your encouragement and the opportunities you have given me. A mentor and a true friend. Cheers then. To Luke Hasell who has always shown his support and trusted in Megan and me to run the business.

To the Root team, past and present; without you all this book would not be here. This book has only been possible through our combined ideas and passion for it all. Special thank you to Jordan for working and at times living with me through the years. To Alfie and Josh: your collective creativity and drive is the reason Root is where it is today. And to Mirai and James; I really do have a dream team: working with you is a pleasure, and thank you for putting up with me through the years. To Marcos, who did the first six months of the restaurant with me and got it off the ground, and what a start it was. It's not only the chefs, but the front of house team who bring the whole place to life. Your spirit and joy makes all the food taste even better; we all know eating at restaurants isn't all about the food, but it's how you feel and who you're with; you guys definitely make the whole experience so much better. So thank you to Billy, Tim, Georgie and Jess, not forgetting Ines and Lidia.

To every chef that I have worked with who have taken the time to teach me and share your kitchens. There are too many to list, but there are definitely a special few that made a real impact. Adam Fellows, Adam Dwyer, Gunther, the team at one 0 one, Roy Brett and the whole team at Ondine – and what a team it was! Special thanks to Dom and Jamie who still inspire me. To the whole Pony & Trap team through all the years, who are all real friends and always will be, the Eggleton family whose support is always there, Jack, Ollie, Joe, Joeby, Nathan, Chris, Boots, Luke. To all the chefs who took the time to come cook with me at little old Root. Thank you Nick Balfe, Jan Ostle, Kirk Haworth, Toby Burrows, Scott Smith, Luke French and John Chantarasak.

To the Bristol chefs who always lead the way in how to do it, together. To Pete and Jonray for giving me the time of day, and for being the ones who told me years and years ago to stick with Josh because he will always look out for me and be a leading man in this industry. To all the restaurants and meals that always made me want to be better, and all the restaurants where we've spent many happy hours: Wilsons, Wallfish, Birch, Adelina Yard, all the Pasta Loco lot, Bertha's and every other outstanding restaurant and food outlet in our city that puts everything they have into it. Got to shout out Farro bakery for out doing us all! To my close friends who have supported and encouraged me from the very start.

Finally, thanks to the suppliers and producers who have made our lives so much more enjoyable with the beautiful produce that surrounds us.

About the author

Having grown up in Somerset, Rob Howell joined the catering industry at the age of 15. He travelled around, gaining experience in kitchens in London, France and Edinburgh before moving closer to home and becoming Head Chef at the Michelin-star-awarded Pony & Trap at just 21. In 2017 he opened Root alongside Josh Eggleton, housed in shipping containers on Bristol's Wapping Wharf, and runs it with his wife, Megan. Here, Rob's vegetable-led menu has been gaining attention since the opening, and was awarded a Bib-Gourmand in 2018.

Rob works with fantastic local ingredients to create simple, honest and produce-driven food. He considers his location in Bristol to be a real advantage, affording him access to exciting produce from the surrounding countryside. Working with a hard-working and passionate team, he ensures that Root's food offering stays unwaveringly fresh, sustainable and, ultimately, delicious.

Publisher
Jon Croft

Commissioning Editor
Meg Boas

Art Direction and Design
Peter Moffat
& Marie O'Shepherd

Junior Designer
Anika Schulze

Senior Project Editor
Emily North

Photographer
Alexander J. Collins

Illustrator
William Walton-Freeman

Copyeditor
Judy Barratt

Proofreader
Margaret Haynes

Home Economist
Elaine Byfield

Indexer
Zoe Ross

BLOOMSBURY ABSOLUTE
Bloomsbury Publishing Plc
50 Bedford Square, London, WC1B 3DP, UK
29 Earlsfort Terrace, Dublin 2, Ireland

BLOOMSBURY, BLOOMSBURY ABSOLUTE, the Diana logo and the
Absolute Press logo are trademarks of Bloomsbury Publishing Plc

First published in Great Britain 2021

A catalogue record for this book is available from the British Library.

Library of Congress Cataloguing-in-Publication data has been applied for.

HB: 9781472976468
ePub: 9781472976475
ePDF: 9781472976482

2 4 6 8 10 9 7 5 3

Printed and bound in China by C&C Offset Printing Co.

Bloomsbury Publishing Plc makes every effort to ensure that the papers
used in the manufacture of our books are natural, recyclable products
made from wood grown in well-managed forests. Our manufacturing
processes conform to the environmental regulations of the country
of origin.

To find out more about our authors and books visit www.bloomsbury.com
and sign up for our newsletters.